Hardness of Heart in Biblical Literature

Hardness of Heart in Biblical Literature

—— *Failure and Refusal* ——

Charles. B. Puskas

CASCADE *Books* • Eugene, Oregon

HARDNESS OF HEART IN BIBLICAL LITERATURE
Failure and Refusal

Copyright © 2022 Charles. B. Puskas. All rights reserved. Except for brief quotations in critical publications or reviews, no part of this book may be reproduced in any manner without prior written permission from the publisher. Write: Permissions, Wipf and Stock Publishers, 199 W. 8th Ave., Suite 3, Eugene, OR 97401.

Cascade Books
An Imprint of Wipf and Stock Publishers
199 W. 8th Ave., Suite 3
Eugene, OR 97401

www.wipfandstock.com

PAPERBACK ISBN: 978-1-6667-3650-2
HARDCOVER ISBN: 978-1-6667-9486-1
EBOOK ISBN: 978-1-6667-9487-8

Cataloguing-in-Publication data:

Names: Puskas, Charles. B. [author].

Title: Hardness of heart in biblical literature : failure and refusal / by Charles. B. Puskas.

Description: Eugene, OR: Cascade Books, 2022 | Includes bibliographical references and index.

Identifiers: ISBN 978-1-6667-3650-2 (paperback) | ISBN 978-1-6667-9486-1 (hardcover) | ISBN 978-1-6667-9487-8 (ebook)

Subjects: LCSH: Bible—Theology | Sin—Biblical teaching | Bible—Criticism, interpretation | Repentance | Israel (Christian theology)

Classification: BS680.S57 P87 2022 (print) | BS680.S57 (ebook)

09/09/22

Scripture quotations are from the New Revised Standard Version of the Bible, copyright 1989 by the Division of Christian Education of the National Council of the Churches of Christ in the USA, and used by permission.

Contents

Abbreviations | vii
Preface | xv

Introduction | 1

I. Old Testament | 5
   Lexical Terms and Equivalents   6
   The Hardening of Non-Israelites   8
   The Hardening of Israelites   16

II. New Testament | 33
   Lexical Terms and Equivalents   33
   The Hardening of Gentiles   35
   The Hardening of Israel   36
   The Hardening of Believers   45

Conclusion | 50

Appendix: On Natural and Grafted Branches (Romans 11:17–24): Israel and the Church in Robert Jenson's *Systematic Theology*, Ancillary or Necessary Concern? | 61

Bibliography | 77
Author Index | 103
Ancient Document Index | 107

Abbreviations

Abbreviations for journals (*JBL*, *NTS*), periodicals (BA), major reference works (*NIDB*), and series (LCL, NIGTC) follow those of *The SBL Handbook of Style: for Ancient Near Eastern, Biblical and Early Christian Studies*, 2nd ed., B. J. Collins, Project Director, et al. Atlanta: SBL Press, 2014, and also *The Chicago Manual of Style*. 15th ed. Chicago: University of Chicago Press, 2003. I cite the abbreviations below that are most frequently used in my book.

Modern Publications and Series

ANF	*The Ante-Nicene Fathers*. Edited by Alexander Roberts and James Donaldson. 1885–87. 10 vols. Reprint, Peabody, MA: Hendrickson, 1994
ACNT	Augsburg Commentary of the New Testament. Minneapolis, MN
ANRW	*Aufstieg uns Niedergang der römischen Welt*. Berlin: de Gruyter, 1972–
AYB	Anchor Yale Bible
AYBD	*Anchor Yale Bible Dictionary*. Edited by D. N. Freedman. 6 vols. New Haven: Yale University Press, 1992
BDAG	Bauer, Danker, Arndt, and Gingrich, eds. *A Greek-English Lexicon of the New Testament and Other Early Christian Literature*. Chicago: University of Chicago Press, 2000
BDB	*Brown-Driver-Briggs Hebrew and English Lexicon* (1907)

ABBREVIATIONS

BHS	*Biblia Hebraica Stuttgartensia.* Stuttgart: Deutsche Bibelgesellschaft, 1997
CBQ	*Catholic Biblical Quarterly*
DOTP	*Dictionary of the Old Testament: Pentateuch.* Downers Grove, IL: IVP, 2003
DSS	Dead Sea Scrolls
EncJud	*Encyclopedia Judaica.* 16 vols. Jerusalem: Macmillan, 1972
EDEJ	*Eerdmans Dictionary of Early Judaism.* Edited by J. J. Collins et al. Grand Rapids: Eerdmans, 2010
FOTL	The Forms of the Old Testament Literature
GKC	*Gesenius' Hebrew Grammar.* Edited by H. Gesenius, E. Kautzsch, and A. Cowley. Oxford: Oxford University Press, 1922
HALOT	*Hebrew and Aramaic Lexicon of the Old Testament.* Edited by Ludwig Koehler et al. Leiden: Brill, 1994–2000
ICC	International Critical Commentary
IDBSupp	*The Interpreter's Dictionary of the Bible, Supplementary Volume.* Nashville: Abingdon, 1976
JANT	*Jewish Annotated New Testament,* eds. A.-J. Levine and M. Z. Brettler. New York: Oxford University Press, 2011.
JBL	*Journal of Biblical Literature*
JEA	*Journal Egyptian Archaeology*
JETS	*Journal of the Evangelical Theological Society*
JSJ	*Journal for the Study of Judaism*
JSNT	*Journal for the Study of the New Testament*
LCL	Loeb Classical Library. Cambridge: Harvard University Press
LSJ	H. G. Liddell, R. Scott, and H. S. Jones, eds. *A Greek-English Lexicon.* Oxford: Oxford University Press, 1983
NA^{28}	*Novum Testamentum Graece.* 28th ed. by Nestle and Aland et al. Stuttgart: Deutsche Bibelgesellschaft, 2012
NAC	New American Commentary. Nashville: Broadman & Holman
NET Bible	The NET Bible. 2007. www.bible.org

ABBREVIATIONS

NETS	*A New English Translation of the Septuagint.* Oxford: Oxford University Press, 2007
NHL	Nag Hammadi Library
NIB	*New Interpreter's Bible.* 12 vols. Nashville: Abingdon, 1994–2004
NICNT	New International Commentary of the New Testament
NICOT	New International Commentary of the Old Testament
NIDB	*New Interpreter's Dictionary of the Bible.* 5 vols. Nashville: Abingdon, 2006
NIV	New International Version
NJB	New Jerusalem Bible
NJPS	Tanakh: The Holy Scriptures. The New JPS translation
NLT	New Living Translation. Tyndale House
NovT	*Novum Testamentum*
NRSV	New Revised Standard Version
NTS	*New Testament Studies*
OCD	*Oxford Classical Dictionary.* Oxford University Press, 2012
PRSt	*Perspectives in Religious Studies*
RB	*Revue biblique*
RGRW	Religions in the Greco-Roman World
RevQ	*Revue de Qumran*
RSV	Revised Standard Version
SBLDS	Society of Biblical Literature Dissertation Series
SNTMS	*Society of New Testament Monograph Series*
ST	*Systematic Theology,* by Robert W. Jenson. 2 vols. Oxford: Oxford University Press, 2001
SUNT	*Studien zur Umwelt des Neuen Testaments*
TDNT	*Theological Dictionary of the New Testament.* 10 vols. Edited by Gerhard Kittel et al. Grand Rapids: Eerdmans, 1964–76
TDOT	*Theological Dictionary of the Old Testament.* 17 vols. Edited by Helmer Ringgren et al. Grand Rapids: Eerdmans, 1975–2018
TJ	*Trinity Journal*

ABBREVIATIONS

TPI	Trinity Press International
WJK	Westminster John Knox
WBC	Word Biblical Commentary
WUNT	Wissenschaftliche Untersuchungen zum Neuen Testament
ZNW	Zeitschrift für die neutestamentliche Wissenschaft

Books of the Bible

Col	Colossians
1–2 Chron	1-2 Chronicles
1–2 Cor	1-2 Corinthians
Dan	Daniel
Deut	Deuteronomy
Eccl	Ecclesiastes
Eph	Ephesians
Exod	Exodus
Ezek	Ezekiel
Gal	Galatians
Gen	Genesis
Heb	Hebrews
Hos	Hosea
Isa	Isaiah
Jas	James
Jer	Jeremiah
John	Gospel of John
Josh	Joshua
Judg	Judge
1–2	1–2 John
1–2 Kgs	1-2 Kings
Luke	Gospel of Luke
Mark	Gospel of Mark

ABBREVIATIONS

Matt	Gospel of Matthew
Mic	Micah
1–2 Pet	1–2 Peter
Phil	Philippians
Prov	Proverbs
Ps(s)	Psalms
Rev	Revelation
Rom	Romans
1–2 Sam	1–2 Samuel
1–2 Thess	1–2 Thessalonians
1–2 Tim	1–2 Timothy
Zech	Zechariah

Apocrypha and Old Testament Pseudepigrapha

2 Bar.	2 Baruch (Syriac Apocalypse)
3 Bar.	2 Baruch (Greek Apocalpse)
1 En	1 Enoch (Ethiopic Enoch)
2 En.	2 Enoch (Slavonic Apocalypse)
3 En.	3 Enoch (Hebrew Apocalypse)
2 Esd	2 Esdras
1–2 Macc	1–2 Maccabees
Odes	Odes of Solomon
Pss. Sol.	Psalms of Solomon
Sir	Sirach/Ecclesiasticus
T. Adam	Testament of Adam
Wis	Wisdom of Solomon

Rabbinica and Targumim

m.	Mishnah
b.	Babylonian Talmud

y.	Jerusalem Talmud
Ber.	Berakot
Ketub.	Ketubbot
Meg.	Megillah
Mek.	Mekilta
Pesaḥ.	Pesaḥim
Sifre	Sifra or Sipre
Tanḥ	Tanḥuma
Tg. Ket.	Targum Ketubim (Targum Writings)
Tg. Neb.	Targum Nebiim (Targum Prophets)
Tg. Onq.	Targum Onqelos
Tg. Ps.-J.	Targum Pseudo-Jonahtan
Yad.	Yadayim
Zebaḥ.	Zebaḥim

Dead Sea Scrolls (DSS) and Related Texts

CD	Cairo Genizah copy of the Damascus Document
1Q	Qumran Cave 1
1QpHab	Pesher Habakkuk
1QIsa^a	Isaiah^a (HT from Lexham Press, 2010)
1QM	Milḥamah or War Scroll
1QS	Serek Hayaḥad, or Rule of the Community
4Q	Qumran Cave 4
4QFlor	Florilegium, or Midrash on Eschatology
4Q254	Commentary on Genesis

Other Writings of Antiquity

Ap. John	Apocryphon of John (Secret Book of John)
Corp. herm.	Corpus hermeticum
Euripides, *Bacch.*	*Bacchae* (*Bacchanals*)

Eusebius, *Hist. eccl.*	*Historia ecclesiastica*
Herm. *Man.*	Shepherd of Hermas, Mandates (older numbering: 7.1)
Herm. Sim.	Shepherd of Hermas, Similitudes (8.7.6)
Hippolytus, *Haer.*	*Refutatio omium haeresium*
Hyp. Arch.	Nature of the Rulers
Ign. *Pol.*	Ignatius, *To Polycarp*
Ign. *Smyrn.*	Ignatius, *To the Smyrnaeans*
Josephus, *Ant.*	*Jewish Antiquities*
Josephus, *J.W.*	*Jewish War*
Justin, *1 Apol.*	Justin Martyr, *First Apology*
Philo, *Opif.*	*De opificio mundo* (On the Creation of the World)
Plato, *Symp.*	Plato, *Symposium*
Protr.	*Protrepticus* (Exhortation to the Greeks) by Clement of Alexandria
Three Forms	Three Forms of First Thought (Trimorphic Protennoia)

General Abbreviations

adj.	adjective
adv.	adversus
Aram.	Aramaic
AT	Author Translation
BCE	before the Common Era
bk(s).	book(s)
ca.	circa "around, about"
CE	Common Era
cent.	Century
cf.	*confer*, compare
ch(s).	chapter(s)
ed(s).	editor(s); edition; edited by

ABBREVIATIONS

Eng.	English
ET	English translation
ep.	epistula
e.g.	*exempli gratia*, for example
esp.	especially
et al.	*et alii*, and others
fr.	fragmentum, fragmenta
Ger.	German
Gk.	Greek
Heb.	Hebrew
HT	Hebrew text
IMV	imperative mood
Ind.	Indicative mood
i.e.	*id est*, that is
Lat.	Latin
MT	Masoretic Text of Hebrew Bible
n	note
n.s.	new series
NT	New Testament
par(r).	parallel(s)
pl.	plural
OT	Old Testament
repr.	reprinted
rev.	revised
sing.	singular
trans.	translated by
vs.	versus
v(v).	verse(s)
vol(s).	volume(s)

Preface

THIS BOOK IS A thoroughgoing revision of earlier research completed in partial fulfillment of the comprehensive exam for my doctoral program at Saint Louis University. The theme had interested me because it is included in Acts 28:26–28, quoting Isaiah 6:9–10, a key text in my doctoral dissertation: "The Conclusion of Luke-Acts: The Literary Function and Theological Significance of Acts 28:16–31," published as Charles B. Puskas, *The Conclusion of Luke-Acts* (Pickwick, 2009). The dissertation was written under the direction of the Rev. Dr. Robert F. O'Toole, S.J., my Doktorvater, who also read the proofs of my revision. It is to him that this current book is dedicated.

The hardness of heart pronouncement has always intrigued me: Who initiated it? Why was it uttered? By whom, to whom, and for what reason? Of what does this unreceptivity consist? Can a "change of heart" take place?

The appendix to this book is derived from an academic paper that I delivered at the Upper Midwest Regional Meeting of the *AAR/SBL/ASOR*, Luther Seminary, St. Paul, April 4–5, 2014. I have included it here, because the issues discussed there are directly related to Israel's hardening and the incorporation of the church in God's history of salvation highlighted in Romans 9–11.

A productive lexical-thematic study benefits from both the synchronic (literary context) and diachronic (historical development) approaches.[1] Because this motif is found in texts (biblical and extrabiblical),

---

1. Ferdinand de Saussure, *Course in General Linguistics*, 80–81 cited in Thiselton,

PREFACE

I have also sought to understand the world of the text (lexical semantics, narrative, rhetoric, intertextuality), with attention to the world behind the text (sources, traditions, redactions), and consideration for the world in front of the text (e.g., ideal reader, reception history).[2] Other interdisciplinary approaches have been included (psychological, sociological, philosophical, theological). Special thanks to my readers for their input and suggestions: Mark Reasoner, Roy Harrisville, III, Edgar Kellenberger, Matthew Neumann, David Penchansky, Robert F. O'Toole, S.J. Many thanks to my editor, Robin Parry, for recommending my book for publication. I remain responsible for all of its final contents.

Thiselton on Hermeneutics, 197-98.

2. Tate, *Biblical Interpretation*, xv-xxi, 173-212; on the significance of and post-modern challenges to this well-known three-dimensional approach, see Thiselton, *Thiselton on Hermeneutics*, 607-24, 635-38.

Introduction

WHAT IS THIS HARDNESS of heart phenomena of which Scripture speaks? Is it a breakdown in communication,[1] or is it something else? Sometimes the people addressed are noncompliant—for a variety of different reasons, sin being one of them. At the same time there may also be a communication failure involving the messenger, the message, and the intended or ideal audience.

Every speaker, teacher, or preacher has on some occasion encountered an audience that was either unreceptive to or unsympathetic with what he or she had to say. One dominant response to this communication breakdown given by both the prophets of Israel and New Testament authors was to declare that "they have hardened their hearts to the message" or "God has hardened them."

Who became hardened and why? How is this communication failure conveyed? Was it "compensation" for some "deficiency" in communication? What were the (short- or long-term) consequences of such a disposition? Was there any hope for a "change of heart"?

The implications of such a study are not only significant for understanding key issues in biblical criticism and theology, but are relevant for

---

1. I am reminded here of the 1969 Atlantic Records rock song "Communication Breakdown" by Led Zeppelin and also the "failure to communicate" voiced by the captain/warden regarding the noncompliance of the affable convict Lucas Jackson in *Cool Hand Luke*, the 1967 Warner Brothers film based on a novel of the same name by Donn Pearson.

anyone concerned with (a) communication issues between an addresser and addressees[2] and (b) for (illustrative purposes) understanding oppositional behavior and the psychology of resistance.[3]

Amélie Oksenberg Rorty stated well the hardness of heart as a natural propensity among many people:

> Nothing is easier, nothing more natural than sliding the slippery slope to corruption, and from there to the hardened heart that allows people to redescribe their wrong doing so that they can accept it as reasonable and confirm it as justified. This is the banal journey charted by Hannah Arendt, the journey from regretful lapses of decency to unrepentant corruption.[4]

Søren Kierkegaard saw the hardness of heart as related to the sin of double-mindedness (Jas 1:8; 4:8; Ps 12:2; cf. Rom 7:15) and contrary to the purity of heart (Matt 5:8; Ps 86:11; Wis 1:1), which is to will one thing:

> *In truth to will one thing can therefore mean only to will the good*, because any other one thing is not a one thing and the person willing who wills only that must therefore be double-minded, because the one who craves becomes like that which he craves. Or would it be possible that a person by willing evil could will one thing even if it were possible that a person could harden himself to willing only

---

2. When the addressee gets the intended message from the addresser then communication has occurred (whether it is welcomed or rejected). Understanding the social contexts and interrelationships of both the addresser and the addressee is crucial to accomplishing this endeavor. See, e.g., Bell, "Language styles," 145–204; Schober and Clark, "Addresses and Overhearers," 211–32. Reader-response criticism is relevant here: who is the intended or ideal audience? See R. M. Fowler, "What is the 'Reader,'" 5–26; and the classic Fish, *Text in This Class?* On the art of persuasion, see, e.g., Watson and Hauser, *Rhetorical Criticism*.

3. For Freud's explanations with sources, see *Psychoanalysis—Resistances* (freudfile.org). See also Kille, *Psychological Biblical Criticism*. It includes a survey of Freudian, Jungian, and developmental explanations of sin and the fall of humanity (Gen 3) with bibliography.

4. Rorty, "How to Harden Your Heart," 282. Via sees Rorty's view here "explained by the dynamic patterns of ordinary psychological activity," *Tragic Finitude*, 218.

Harrisville, argues that not only the Schutzstaffel (SS), but the common soldier was responsible for the myth of the Wehrmacht, promoting it as an honorable institution, whereas in reality the army engaged in atrocities throughout the war. In order for the soldiers to maintain their self-respect they had to believe, and make the home front believe, that what they were doing was for the better. They had to justify their cruelty so they could sleep at night. See his *The Virtuous Wehrmacht*.

evil? Is not evil, just like evil people, at odds with itself, divided in itself?[5]

Kierkegaard's plea is for genuine openness and honesty. It is a striving for betterment, and not a struggle to reach some unattainable "ego ideal" (see my note 5). It is a challenge to stop leading a double life of false pretense that is insincere and dishonest.

For Friedrich Schleiermacher, *Gemüth* (rather than *Herz*) is used to convey the pious heart. "The religious or pious person is the one who has an open heart—a harmonious and integrated interior life that is so because it is also finely attuned to its world and receptive to the divine activity working in and through that world."[6] There can also exist in the heart (*Gemüth* again) preparations for sin, a heart far from God (cf. Mark 7:6; Isa 29:13), that is impious, unattuned, narrow-minded, one-sided, and isolated.[7]

The hardening phenomena in the biblical literature[8] surfaces in different ways with different expressions. All of them seem to concern some theological or ethical problem or crisis. In my study I will indicate the following occurrences. Non-Israelites are usually hardened as enemy "stand-ins" so that YHWH[9] can carry out God's *Heilsgeschichte*[10] in and for Israel.

---

5. Kierkegaard, *Upbuilding Discourses* XV:34. See also "The Divided Self" in James, *Varieties*, 171–75, citing Rom 7:15 and Augustine's *Confessions*, Bk.VIII, chs. 5, 7, 11. See also Sir 1:28; 1 En. 91:4.
Could such striving for a "pure heart" lead to "a sense of guilt unfounded in reality ("metaphysical guilt"), the tyrannical "ego ideal" of artificial perfection described by psychologist Horney, and hostility toward a fallen world"? See Bechtel, "Genesis 2.4b—3.24," 3–26; Horney, *Inner Conflicts*. Summary from Kille, *Psychological Biblical Criticism*, 122.

6. Quotations from Lamm, *Schleiermacher*, 57–58. "*Gemüth* carries a range of meanings similar to *Geist* and *Seele* (mind, spirit, soul, heart), referring to the interior; to the seat of one's feelings and basic disposition, and thus to the defining characteristics of the whole person." Ibid., 57. *Herz* is the more frequently used German word for "heart, breast, bosom, mind, spirit."

7. Lamm, *Schleiermacher*, 96n203, 243, 247 (scattered references to the impious heart). Although the introspective self is a modernist notion (cf. Taylor, *Sources of the Self*) Schleiermacher's insights on the heart resonate with key biblical texts, his eisegesis here is minimal, in my opinion.

8. I use the phrase "biblical literature," to denote the Hebrew Bible, the Deuterocanonical writings, the New Testament, and relevant extrabiblical literature.

9. The Tetragrammaton, a series of the four consonants, YHWH/יהוה, traditionally written without vowels (NRSV, LORD), because God's name is not to be pronounced aloud, see Perdue, "Names of God, "685; *HALOT*, 394–95.

10. I realize that *die Heilsgeschichte* is a loaded concept, cognizant of the criticisms of Franz Hesse, Petr Pokorny, and Rudolf Bultmann, but I believe that Oscar Cullmann's

When the extreme apostasy of certain individuals among God's people is unexplainable on a natural level the conclusion is that "God hardened them," and when God's people become so fixed in unbelief and doubt in response to proclaimers of God's Word, the conclusion is, "God hardened them." This hardening motif was used extensively by OT prophets and NT evangelists as an effective device for addressing both theological and ethical problems in their respective communities. In some cases it can be a self-hardening of the people, in other cases the divine causality is direct ("God hardened them") or indirect ("their hearts *were* hardened").

In agreement with the view of Gerhard von Rad, that a consistent tradition-history of hardness of heart is difficult, I will attempt to survey the history of the hardening phenomena in both the OT and NT with special attention to the activity of God and its effects on the people in the theology of the biblical writers. A representative selection of passages, biblical and extrabiblical, will be used in this survey.

---

version, *Salvation in History*, still has some merit, as long as the tensions between Israel's history and the Christ-event are recognized, see discussion in Reventlow, "Theology (Biblical)," 497–98. See also Goldingay, *Theological Diversity*.

I

Old Testament

WHEN I MENTION THE Old Testament (OT) I refer to the thirty-six books as listed in the *Biblia Hebraica*.[1] The contents are the same as the twenty-four books of the Jewish canon (2 Esd 14:45–47), but with different book designations that make its list longer. I also include the Septuagint, a Greek translation of the OT, that includes books *outside* the Hebrew Bible (e.g., 1–4 Maccabees, Sirach, Tobit, Wisdom of Solomon, Ps 151), called the OT Apocrypha or Deutero-canonical writings (OT books that are in the Catholic and Orthodox Bibles).[2]

In my preface I stated that a productive lexical-thematic study benefits from both the synchronic (literary context) and diachronic (historical

---

1. This list of books is the same as the thirty-nine-book Protestant canon (see NRSV, OT), but in the table of contents of the *Biblia Hebraica Stuttgartensia*: "Samuel" includes 1 and 2 Samuel, "Reges" includes 1 and 2 Kings, and "Chronica" 1 and 2 Chronicles. All three double volumes are listed as single volumes, totaling thirty-six, not thirty-nine. On the different numberings of the Hebrew Bible: Law, Prophets, and Writings (e.g., twenty-two in Josephus, *Ag. Ap.* 1.37–41; twenty-four in 4 Ezra 14:45–47) and the open-ended nature of the OT canon with LXX and DSS, see Collins, "Canon," 460–63. See also Trebolle, "Canon of OT," 548–63, esp. 550–51.

2. The following books are in the Greek and Slavonic Bibles, but *not* in the Roman Catholic canon: 1 Esdras (2 Esdras in Slavonic Bible); Prayer of Manasseh; Ps 151; 3 Maccabees. The Ethiopian Church also includes 1 Enoch and Jubilees. See McDonald, "Forming Jewish Scriptures," 71–96; Stuckenbruck, "Apocrypha and Pseudepigrapha," 143–62. For LXX I follow and include what is found in Rahlfs et al. *Septuaginta*. I note relevant LXX Greek texts in this chapter as they relate to my discussion of the Hebrew terms.

development) approaches.[3] The hardness of heart motif is focused on words and the meanings they denote in context. The three levels of my lexical-thematic analysis are "at the level of individual words, or at the sentence level, or at the level of discourse. These levels are so closely interrelated that to isolate one of them . . . is somewhat artificial and ultimately unsatisfactory."[4] The challenge for both synchronic and diachronic approaches to words in the text is understanding them in their proper literary and historical contexts with special consideration given to their distinct understandings in the ancient Near East and Greco-Roman contexts. I am familiar with the hasty comparisons and contrasts that have been made between Hebrew and Greek thought and the project of developing a synchronic theology from linguistic analysis with little attention to diachronic study. The challenge is doing justice to a complex theme that stretches from the tenth century, BCE to the second century, CE, respecting "*Gattung* and *Sitz im Leben*."[5]

Lexical Terms and Equivalents[6]

The hardening terminology comes to expression in many ways, some key terms are:

---

3. Saussure, *General Linguistics*, 80–81, cited in *Thiselton on Hermeneutics*, 197–98.

4. Quote from Silva, *Biblical Words*, 11.

5. German phrase regarding "form and setting in life" (ET) is from *Thiselton on Hermeneutics*, 196. Note also the caution expressed by James Barr on the contrast of Hebrew and Greek thought, as well as gleaning theology from linguistic analysis that ignores context, *Biblical Words for Time* and "Common Sense," 377–87; and his *Semantics*, especially his focus on syntactical relations and the groupings of words at the sentence level, 222, 249–50, 69–70. See also Penchansky, *Biblical Theology*; Silva, *Biblical Words* (cited earlier, n4).

6. For Hebrew text (MT) I use the *Biblia Hebraica Stuttgartensia*. The following works have been helpful in this section of study: *HALOT*; GKC; Hesse, *Das Verstockungsproblem*; *TDOT*.

kabēd—כָּבֵד Qal and Hiphil "to make hard or heavy" ("ears," *ōzen* אֹזֶן Isa 6:10; 1QS IV, 11)⁷

ḥāzaq חָזַק—in the piel stem, "to become strong, hard" ("heart" *lēb*, לֵב Exod 4:21; 10:20)⁸

qāshâ קָשָׁה—*hipil* "to be stiff, hard" ("heart," Exod 7:3; Isa 63:17; "neck" *ōrep* עֹרֶף Jer 17:23); *qəshê-pānîm*—קְשֵׁי פָנִים "stiff-faced" (Ezek 2:4); *qəshê 'ōrep* קְשֵׁה עֹרֶף (Exod 33:3, 5) "stiff-necked"

āmētz—אָמֵץ piel, "to be hard, firm" ("heart," Deut 2:30; 15:7)⁹

mārâ מָרָה Qal "to be rebellious" (Deut 31:27; Isa 1:20; Ezek 3:9)

sārar—סָרַר "stubborn" (Ps 78:8; apostasy? Isa 1:23; 65:2; 1QHa XIII, 24; CD-A XI, 7); *lēb sôrēr ûmôreh* לֵב סוֹרֵר וּמוֹרֶה "stubbornness and rebellious heart" (Jer 5:23)

shərirût שְׁרִרוּת "stubborn, stubbornnness" (Deut 29:19; Jer 16:12; 1QS III, 3)

'erel lēb wə'erel bāsār עֲרֵל לֵב וְעֲרֵל בָּשָׂר "uncircumcised/having foreskin of heart and uncircumcised/having foreskin of flesh" (Ezek 44:7, 9), applied to foreign attendants in the temple. In LXX it is translated here *aperitmētos* ἀπερίτμητος "uncircumcised" instead of *akrobustia* ἀκροβυστία "foreskin" (cf. Gen 17:14 LXX).

The diverse hardening terminology is metaphorically applied to various parts of the body: the heart (showing disobedience or stubbornness, Exod 8:11; 1QS IV, 11), but also the ears (deaf, failure to listen, Isa 6:10; 59:1; Zech 7:11), the eyes (lack of perception, Gen 48:10),¹⁰ the face and

---

7. Although the above terminology function in similar ways in the narrative, the primary meaning of *kābēd* as "heavy" (adj., Exod 7:14) has significance here. "According to Egyptian belief, the gods Anubis and Thoth weighed and recorded the weight of a person's heart after death. If the heart was light, its possessor was ushered into eternal life. If the heart was heavy with misdeeds, Amemit stood by to consume the individual," Cox, "Hardening of Pharaoh's Heart," 305n39 citing, e.g., Currid, *Ancient Egypt*, 96–98; his "Why Did God Harden Pharaoh's Heart?" 47–51, and Silverman, *Ancient Egypt*, 132–47. See also Kellenberger, *Die Verstockung Pharaos*, 8, 11–12; Steinmann, "Hardness of Heart," 382.

8. Dozeman mentions that *ḥāzaq* חָזַק is used to describe *both* the "might" of YHWH (Exod 13:9; 32:11) and the "hardened" heart of Pharaoh (7:22; 8:15), in his *Exodus*, 138–39.

9. The phrase *ametz lēb*, used twice in Deuteronomy and three times in OT, denotes a positive posture in Pss 27:14 (Hiphil); 31:24 (MT 31:25): "let your heart be firm/take courage."

10. It is a depletion of the senses of hearing and seeing as seen in Isa 6:9–10.

forehead (lack of response, Jer 5:3; Ezek 2:4; 3:7–9), the neck (Exod 33:5),[11] shoulder, and back (Exod 34:9; Deut 9:6; *sārar kathēph*, "stubborn shoulder," Zech 7:11; 2 Chr 30:8; Neh 9:16–17, 29, symbols of insubordination, cf. Hos 4:16).[12] All three hardening verbs (*ḥāzaq, kābēd, qāshâ*) are used in Exodus 7 (Exod. 7:3, 13, 14, 22) and convey a similar meaning.[13] The hardness of heart motif concerns the failure and refusal to understand. It finds its meaning and significance in its literary relationship to the above words and images with some understanding of their historical development.

The Hardening of Non-Israelites

Does an early source (J or Yahwist) behind the hardening of Pharaoh in the Book of Exodus reflect a particular time in Israel's history? Could this superior attitude of Israel to the nations (here Egypt) reflect a period when it faced no nation greater than itself (eleventh to tenth centuries BCE)? Even the references to the hardening of Egyptians do not depict Egypt as the mighty power of the eighteenth and nineteenth dynasties but as the struggling nation of the eleventh century (e.g., Exod. 12:36; 15:4). It has been proposed by some that it wasn't until the eighth century, when the emerging power of Assyria came on the scene (e.g., 2 Kgs 15:19–20), that this superior attitude of Israel began to wane. The above view is based

---

11. The metaphor of the neck (Hebrew *ōrep* עֹרֶף Exod 33:5; Isa 48:4; Jer 7:26), "the part of the animal body that connects the head to the backbone, is taken from the draft animal, whose efforts to resist are localized in the neck, Gk. σκληροκαρδία, σκληρός" Spicq and Ernest, *Theological Lexicon 3*, 260. In Deut 28:48; Jer 28:14, prisoners wear around the "neck" (Heb. *tsawəwā'r* צַוָּאר) a "yoke of iron" (*ōl barzel* עֹל בַּרְזֶל), whereas draft animals would wear a wooden yoke. In Ps 105:18 "his neck (Heb. *nephesh* נֶפֶשׁ) was in [a collar of] iron" (Joseph, a slave in Egypt). See also LXX Ps 104:18, *psychē* ψυχή. In both texts the idea of "neck" seems to be conveyed. In (seventh cent. CE) Qur'an 40 Sūrat al-Ghāfir (the Forgiving One), men in hell have iron collars on their necks (Q 40.71). See Penchansky, *Solomon and the Ant*, 75.

12. This cluster of images, e.g., blindness, deafness, stiffness, covering a range of attitudes, e.g., refusal to listen, inability to understand, irrationality, and rebelliousness, is surveyed in "Harden, Hardness," Leland Ryken et al., *Biblical Imagery*, 364. Studies of metaphor will help to clarify the figurative language, see, e.g., Lakoff and Johnson, *Metaphors*. Also, the study of the interrelationship of body, movement, affect, and sensation may prove useful in the interpretation of this biblical theme of hardening, see, e.g., Massumi, *Parables for the Virtual*.

13. Steinmann, "Hardness of Heart," 381.

on an early "Solomonic" source (J) for the Book of Exodus, which has been challenged in recent decades.[14]

The hardening of Pharaoh and the Egyptians.

The general period of the exodus is the New Kingdom era of Egypt. Here, the key figures chronologically are Amenhotep (Amenophis) I and particularly: Thutmose III (eighteenth dynasty), and Rameses II (nineteenth dynasty). "From the reign of Thutmose III we have a lunar date which would imply his accession to the throne in 1479 BCE, corresponding to datum from the reign of Rameses II, favoring his accession in 1279 BCE, in conjunction (1) with synchronisms from other Near Eastern rulers and (2) with the lapse of generations linking the Rameside period to later epochs."[15]

It has been argued that the narrative material of Exodus 1–15 focuses on the Passover (Pesach) ceremony and the feast of unleavened bread celebrated by Israel, in some manner, since pre-monarchial times (tenth century, BCE, or earlier). The hardening motif is located in this context.[16]

If one follows Martin Noth's tradition-historical methodology here, the earliest account of the Exodus "plagues" was the killing of the first born, perhaps recalling ancient fertility rites of the shepherds. Before leaving for summer pastures in the spring the shepherds would kill a firstborn animal to insure fertility of the flocks. Taken over by the Israelites, this was probably incorporated into a Passover feast where the moving out of the shepherds was transferred to the leaving of Egypt. Afterwards, the plagues may have been added as an introduction to this final "plague" so as to bring it to a climax in the narrative. The Exodus account has a sequence of ten plagues

---

14. The statements reflect the pan-Israelite perspective of the Yahwist advocated by Gerhard von Rad and Martin Noth (e.g., Gen 9:26; 15:18; 25:23; 27:37, 40; Num 24:15–19), but the nature of the source and its early date have been challenged by Rendtdorff and others, see discussion in de Pury, "Yahwist Source," 6:1012–20. Coates has observed that the Book of Exodus contains episodes of history, reflecting wisdom about history, rather than historiography, *Exodus*, 11.

15. Kitchen, "Egypt," 2:327. See also Hoffmeier, *Israel in Egypt*; See also his argument for a thirteenth-century BCE date for the exodus in Janzen, *Five Views*, 21–22, 103–8, and supportive review by Rendsburg, "Response to James K. Hoffmeier," 121–23; see also Hawkins, *Israel Became a People*.

16. Coats, discusses the blending of earlier agricultural traditions of unleavened bread and the first born with the later Passover and the exodus traditions (dominant in P), *Exodus*, 83–85. On discussion of origins, see also Bokser, "Unleavened Bread," 6:759–63 (755–65).

(Exod 7:14—12:30), only seven plagues are later mentioned in the more poetic Psalms 78:42–51; 105:28–36. Noth's tradition-historical interpretation, however, lacks sufficient data to support its claim.[17]

Franz Hesse, seeks an explanation from oral-transmission history. Hesse suggests that it was out of the joy of storytelling that the hardening of Pharaoh was added to the plagues (ancient boycotts?). As the storyteller would describe those exciting plague stories, the question was raised: "Why could not Yahweh stop Pharaoh with one plague?" The reply of the storyteller: "Yahweh hardened Pharaoh so that he could not obey."[18] "Hence the power of Yahweh is vindicated and the storyteller could continue his plague stories." I add a comment from Juvenal (second century CE) on the delay of heaven to act. It follows the discussion in his *Satires* about those who would *not* fear to perjure themselves on the altar of the gods. Juvenal then cites those who would rationalize the situation: "though it may be great, the wrath of the gods is certainly slow" (Bk. 5, XIII.100).[19]

There is little agreement on reconstructing the history of the hardening motif within Israel's oral and literary traditions. The theme occurs twenty times between Exod 4:21 (Pharaoh is hardened) and Exod 14:17 (the Egyptians are hardened) and is an important constituent of the plague, Passover, and crossing narratives. Because the hardening motif is so extensive in Exodus 4–14, interpreters have argued that it was (1) a literary device providing some coherence (U. Cassuto), (2) the creation of the authors or editors to link together the sequence of the plagues (G.

---

17. "The sober fact remains that *no* extrabiblical original or relevant background for the Passover celebration has so far been discovered; all suggestions about origins are guesswork at present," Kitchen, *"Exodus,"* 2:705 (700–708). For more discussion of the Passover and related traditions, see Childs, *Exodus* (1974), 189–201. On the selectivity of the number of plagues in the Psalms, see deClaissé-Walford et al., *Psalms*, 792.

18. Rashi (ca. 1100) has speculated that perhaps God had "strengthened" *ḥāzaq* Pharaoh's heart (Exod 4:21; 9:12; 10:20; 11:10; 14:4, and that of Egyptians, v. 17) to endure this long contest of ten plagues with the Creator of the world who would get glory over the gods of Egypt and thus all would know that YHWH is the true God (14:4). See Moshe Dann, jpost.com. 22:03; also Munk, *Call of Torah*, 84. This attribute of strength, however, is reserved for YHWH (Exod 13:9, *ḥāzaq* "strong, hard"; LXX *krataios* κραταιός "might, power;" 9:16; 15:6; 32:11 "strength, power," *kōaḥ* כֹּחַ; LXX *ischus*, ἰσχύς; same language in Deut 4:37; 9:29). Coates, citing Eising, sees the hard-heart motif as a transition to the following scene, *Exodus*, 66–67.

19. Latin: *ut sit magna, tamen certe lenta ira deorum est* in Juvenal *Saturae* XIII.100, 252–53.

Forhrer), and (3) added later to explain why the divine signs failed to achieve their purpose (B. Childs).[20]

In Exodus, the hardening language is chiefly connected with the heart, e.g., "Pharaoh hardened his heart" (Exod. 8:32 ET). "Heart" (*lēb*), is an important anthropological term here and in the OT. It occurs over 850 times. Most of the passages connect *lēb* with different aspects of the inner life such as "feelings," "emotionality," and "sensibility." Rarely does *lēb* mean the physical organ (e.g., 1 Sam 25:37; 2 Kgs 9:24).[21] Included in the symbolic use are passages that refer to "courage" or its counterpart "fear." When courage is lacking, the heart is like leaves in the wind (Isa 7:2), it becomes soft and weak (Isa 7:4; Deut 20:8), dissolves like wax (Deut 8:20; Ps 22:15) or water (Josh 7:5). In addition, *lēb* has a more intellectual or rational function (cf. Deut 29:3) and can play a volitional role as in decision-making.[22] In ancient Egyptian culture, the heart is at the center of one's personality.[23] Tertullian of Carthage (ca. 200 CE), citing ancient Egypt in support, also viewed the heart as a vital, guiding faculty (*De Anima* 15.5).[24]

The phrases meaning "to harden the heart" do not *often* occur outside of Exodus 4–14, nor in biblical Hebrew. Akkadian and Ugaritic also rarely speak of the hardened heart. However, ancient Egyptian does contain several expressions meaning "to be hard of heart." So *mn ib*, literally "firm of heart," means "constant, persevering, obstinate, headstrong, defiant"; *rwd ib*, literally "hard of heart," means "persistent, stout-hearted, unyielding";

---

20. The views of Cassuto and Childs appeal to me. For more discussion, see Wilson, "The Hardening of Pharaoh's Heart," 19–21. On form and structure, see Coats, *Exodus*.

21. Proceeding with *lēb* as a physical organ and following a literal meaning of *ḥāzaq* and *qāshâ*, references to the "hardening" of Pharaoh's heart (Exod 4:21; 7:3) have been taken to represent coronary arteriosclerosis, See Cameron, "The Bible and Legal Medicine," 7–13, an *odd* study cited in Sussman, "Sickness and Disease," 14. Knowing today that our heart pump is *not* the seat of emotions, does not always safeguard it from becoming emotion's victim, see Rosenbaum, *How Emotions Affect Your Health*, how, e.g., stress and guilt can lead to psychosomatic heart problems.

22. Wünch, "The Strong and the Fat Heart," 165–88, citing discussion in Wolff and Janowski, *Anthropologie des Alten Testaments*, 82–84, on decision-making, 90–96.

23. Assmann, "des Herzens im Alten Ägypten," 81–113. See also Fabry, "לֵב," *TDOT* 7:401–2.

24. Lat. *Namque homini sanguis circumcordialis est sensus* (citing Gk., Stobaeus *Eclogues* 1). "Man has as his (supreme) sensation the blood around the heart." Holmes. *ANF* Vol. III:194 (tertullian.org).

nht ib, literally "strong of heart," means "to be courageous, confident"; and *dns (dni) ib*, literally "heavy of heart," means "reticent."[25]

Regarding sources, Exodus is a patchwork quilt of traditions from various periods in Israel's life. The epic traditions (J and E) are significantly represented in Exodus 1–24 and 32–34, interwoven also with the Priestly traditions (P) that are more concentrated in chapters (25–31 and 35–40).[26]

The Yahwist (J document) appears to reflect some concern for the succession of the plagues.[27] The plagues are to both punish and soften Pharaoh, but when conditions are normalized Pharaoh hardens his heart and the plagues continue. J uses only the Hebrew term *kābēd* for his hardening of Pharaoh (six times in Exod 10:1–2, a later redaction?).[28] In J a hardening from YHWH is only *implied* (with the passive, "was heavy/hardened," Exod 7:14; 9:7) emphasizing the human response to YHWH's demand (Exod 8:15 [ET]; 8:32).[29] The Septuagint (LXX) uses *sklērynō* σκληρύνω once ("was hardened," Exod 8:15) but mostly *barynō* βαρύνω "weigh down" in Exodus 7:14; 8:28 (NRSV 8:32); 9:7, 34 translated as "was weighed down" (passive voice may *imply* divine influence) similar to the Hebrew *kabēd*, "make heavy" in the so-called J document.[30]

25. Wilson, "Hardening of Pharaoh's Heart," 24n22, citing the following sources: Erman and Grapow, *der aegyptischen Sprache* 2:60–61, 410–11, 314–15; 5:468; Piankoff, "coeur" 34–39, 112, 114, 116, 123; Hintze, "Sethos,'" 35; Clère, "dné mhwt," 38–41; and Shirun-Grumach, *des Ameno*, 125.

26. Fretheim, *Pentateuch*, 101–2. See also Blenkinsopp, *Pentateuch*; Whybray, *Pentateuch*.

27. For a survey of diverse views on the Documentary Hypothesis (J, E, P, D), see Arnold, "Pentateuchal Criticism," 622–31. In my use of the J, E, P, D hypothesis, I follow the classic explanations in Driver, *Introduction*, 23–29; Rogerson, *Old Testament Criticism*, 257–89; I also derive some insights from LaVerdiere, *Pentateuch*; and (more critical of Wellhausen and Driver): Childs, *Exodus* and Dozeman, *Exodus*, 31–41, the latter focusing on "non-P" (J, E, D) and P materials in Exodus, see 40–41.

28. See table showing verb, stem, function, subject, object, possessor, and episode on "the hard of heart" in Exodus in Garrett, *Exodus*, 371. Garrett does not subscribe to the Documentary Hypothesis. See 1 Sam 6:6, where the author, in the ark narrative, also used *kābēd* to recall the self-hardening of Pharaoh and the Egyptians.

29. "It is suggested that the attribution of the hardening to YHWH is due to the mindset of the writers who would attribute everything ultimately to YHWH, but in such a way as *not* to deny the reality and efficacy of proximate causes through human agency." Ford, *God, Pharaoh, Moses*, 8, citing Cassuto, *Exodus*, 55–57; and Driver, *Exodus*, 53–54. Ford, reacting to Cassuto's quote: "This explanation causes a problem if the principle is extended to other acts of YHWH," see *God, Pharaoh, Moses*, 8n35. For more discussion, see his pp. 8–10.

30. For LXX, I use Rahlfs et al., *Septuaginta*. The Latin Vulgate employs two related

The Elohist (E document)[31] seems unconcerned with succession of narratives and that Pharaoh is not swayed by the plagues. E characteristically uses *ḥāzaq* (like the P document's twelve total occurrences in Exod) and refers to *God* hardening Pharaoh (Exod 4:21; passive voice, 9:35, 10:20, 27) perhaps reflecting the prophet's traditions of the northern kingdom (eighth century BCE). The so-called E source appears to have no ethical or theological problems with *God* hardening people.[32] The impending exodus event is a play in which "God is author, producer, director, and principal actor," and the fate of both Israel and Egypt is in God's hand.[33]

The Priestly writer (P document) does not seem to have much concern for the succession of the plague narratives nor that Pharaoh is unconvinced by the plagues. For P, the plagues are "show miracles" so that God's power can be revealed. P always uses *ḥāzaq*, yet appears to recognize the theological tension of Pharaoh's self-hardening (J) and Pharaoh hardened by God (E) and places the two concepts alongside one another in tension (Exod 7:3 [*qāshâ* here], 13, 22; 8:15; 9:12; 11:10; 14:4, 8, 17). Despite the theological complexities of divine foreknowledge (4:21, E?) and human will (7:14, J?), it can be argued that God's hardening of Pharaoh's heart was in response

---

verbs for "make heavy, weigh down," ingravo (Exod 7:14; 9:7) and adgravo ("make heavier," Isa 6:10), see Weber et al., *Vulgata*.

31. The E source has been associated with the prophetic tradition, e.g., Abraham, Aaron, and Miriam are all called prophets (Gen 20:7; Exod 15:20; Num 12:2, 6) and has been associated with the northern kingdom, with its interest in, e.g., Bethel and Shechem (shrines of the north) as well as the patriarchs, Jacob and Joseph, identified with these shrines, see LaVerdiere, *Pentateuch*, 34–41. In his supplementary hypothesis of the Pentateuch, John Van Seters argues against the existence of E as an independent document, and views J and P as direct additions to an earlier corpus, *Abraham*, on J and P, 78, on E, 125–30. Dozeman, *Exodus*, 36, regards E mostly as an addition to J designated as JE or non-P.

32. More famously see Luther's "Bondage of the Will," in Dillenberger, *Martin Luther*, 192, 196–98, and Calvin, *Institutes*, 101–2, 194. Luther's interchange with Erasmus is quite subtle, speaking of the Lord using Pharaoh's evil will to reveal God's power (Kellenberger, *Die Verstockung Pharaos*, 241). Luther notes that the "as the Lord said" rules out any freewill, and Calvin in his *Institutes*, III, 23, vii, seems to dismiss the view that the hardening was in any way permissive. According to Lewis, "the hardness of God is kinder than the softness of man, and His compulsion is our liberation" *Surprised by Joy*. 229. The Lewis quote is certainly true for those whose hearts have been changed.

33. Enns, *Exodus*, 131. On the view that God may allow or grant hardness of heart instead of merely causing it, see Tigay, "Tolerative/Permissive Hiphil," 397–414; Margain, "Causatif et toleratif," 23–31. Although the causative hiphil stem has other nuances (e.g., Exod 12:36; Deut 2:30 NJPS), Joüon and Muraoka have concluded that Margain, for example, has slightly exaggerated the tolerative Hifil, *Biblical Hebrew*, 151n4.

to Pharaoh's prejudicial bias and continual stubbornness (Exod 5:2, 23; cf., *qāsheh* קָשֶׁה 1QS 6:26; Ps 2:1–3/Acts 4:25–28).³⁴ It should also be noted that the P document, the latest source woven into Exodus, adds some final quilt patches to the narrative as we have it.³⁵

In most cases, Pharaoh seems to appear as an enemy "stand-in" so God can carry out salvation-history.³⁶ Is Pharaoh hardened because he does not believe in YHWH?³⁷ This is a minor concern, especially for the Elohist. Pharaoh's main contact with Israel (aside from interviews with Moses and Aaron) is with the saving event of the exodus. Pharaoh is hardened to show God's greatness and is eliminated so *Heilsgeschichte* can continue on.

> The hardening of Pharaoh's heart was also a polemic against the Egyptian belief that Pharaoh's heart was the all-controlling factor in both history and society. The Memphite theology encapsulated on the Shabaka Stone held that the hearts of the gods Re and Horus were sovereign over everything. Because Pharaoh was an incarnation of those two gods, his heart was thought to be sovereign over creation. Yahweh assaulted the heart of Pharaoh to demonstrate

---

34. Hesse, *Das Verstockungsproblem*, 46–51. See comments attributed to R. Yoḥanan in Exod. Rab. 13.1–3 (tenth century CE). See discussion in Steinmann, "Hardness of Heart," 383. See also Weber, "חזק." Feinberg argues for free will within divine causation in this way: "an action is free even if causally determined so long as the causes are non-constraining" (i.e., with no threat of force), see Feinberg, "God Ordains All," 24. For a classic exposition, see Warfield, "PREDESTINATION," 4:47–63. For Eichrodt there is a tension between the divine will and human responsibility for sin (e.g., Exod 20:12; Lev 26:1–2) in his *Theology of the OT* 2:177–81.

35. Johnstone detects some exilic D-material from Deuteronomy and Deuteromomistic traditions (Joshua–2 Kings), *Exodus* 1:187–88 (see also 1–4), but this so-called D-material does not contribute to our discussion of the hardening material in Exodus (as in, e.g., the Decalogue traditions).

36. Pharaoh's actions are in some ways similar to those of Oedipus in the tragedy by Sophocles, *Oedipus Rex* (ca. 430 BCE). The willful actions of both kings lead to their own undoing. See discussion of Oedipus (blindness, hubris, nemesis) in Via, *Tragic Finitude*, 46–52.

37. Is not Pharaoh's hardening his heart against God "akin to the sin of blasphemy of the Holy Spirit" condemned by Jesus in the NT (Mark 3:28–30)? "Even as Jesus' enemies attributed the miraculous works of God to Satan, so Pharaoh in his rejection of God's signs and wonders had willfully denied God's activity in human history. Implicitly Pharaoh attributed the divine works to the demonic by not acknowledging YHWH (Exod 5:2), by calling for counterfeit signs from his magicians (7:11), and by ignoring their discernment of the 'finger of God' intervening in Egyptians history (8:19)." Hill and Walton, *Survey of the OT*, 115. See also Wisdom 10:16, where Moses "a servant of the Lord withstood dreadful kings with signs and wonders," David Winston, *Wisdom of Solomon*, 219.

that only the God of the Hebrews is the sovereign of the universe. That Yahweh controlled the heart of Egypt's king is the basic point of the episode related in Exodus 7:8–13.[38]

Setting aside the Documentary Hypothesis and focusing on the Exodus narrative, there is a "thematic progression" with the hardening motif. It was to show YHWH's power over the Egyptians (Exod 7:17; 8:19; 9:16 [Rom 9:17]; 14:4),[39] to serve as a memorial for Israel and later generations (10:1–2; 13:14–16), and to demonstrate YHWH's glory (כָּבֵד Niphal *kābēd*) over Pharaoh and the Egyptians (14:17–18).[40] The idea of holy war is also evident in YHWH's conflict with Pharaoh.

> Divine involvement also evokes an atmosphere of warfare (cf. Josh 11:20: "For it was the LORD's doing to make their hearts obstinate to meet Israel in battle," but literally, "It was from the LORD to stiffen their heart..."). First Samuel 6:6 cites the hardening of Pharaoh's heart as an object lesson to Israel's enemies, the Philistines.[41]

The above themes also help to explain why we find this "extended sequence" of conflict and contest in Exodus 4–14.[42]

The Hardening of Sihon, the Canaanites, and other Nations

Similar themes occur in Deuteronomy and Joshua where Sihon the Amorite (Deut 2:30 *'āmēts* אָמֵץ)[43] and the Canaanites (Josh 11:20) are hardened so

---

38. Currid, *Ancient Egypt*, 102–3; also citing Beale, "Hardening of Pharaoh's Heart," 149.

39. The Egyptians regarded their god-king, Pharaoh, as responsible for the life-giving Nile River and the sun's daily rising. The plagues, however, indicated that Israel's God, YHWH, was in control of the cosmos. See Hoffmeier, "Egypt, Plagues of," 2:374–78; Hoffmeier, *Israel in Egypt*, 149–55.

40. Beale, "Hardening of Pharaoh's Heart," 149 (129–54). We have noted that כָּבֵד (*kābēd*) denotes "heavy" as well as "glory" see *HALOT*, 455–56. On glory/heavy, see my ch. I, n7. On rabbinical speculation about YHWH making the heart of Pharaoh "strong" to endure his losing contest with the God of Israel, see my ch. I, n18.

41. Smith, *Exodus*, 31. Smith subscribes to a version of the Documentary Hypothesis, detecting the sources of J, E, and P in Exodus.

42. Moberly, "Exodus," 212–13.

43. The victory song in Numbers 21 celebrates Israel's conquest of Sihon's kingdom, an exciting part of Israelite worship: YHWH's victory over Israel's foes. (See also Deut 29:7 where Sihon is again mentioned in the covenant recital.) See Slayton, "Sihon (Person)," 6:22.

that YHWH can perform "holy war" for the sake of Israel. Joshua 11:20 states that the Lord hardened (*ḥāzaq* חָזַק) the hearts of the kings of Canaan so that Joshua could destroy them as Moses had commanded. Both Sihon and the Canaanites were hardened so that they can eventually be eliminated from the picture. Both texts recall Exodus 4:21, and seem to compare Sihon and the Canaanites with Pharaoh and the Egyptians. Their obedience or salvation appears to be of little concern to the Deuteronomist Historian (DtrH).[44] They are merely enemy stand-ins so God can perform *Heilsgeschichte* on behalf of Israel. As it was in the case of Pharaoh, a change of heart is always possible (cf. Rahab, Josh 2:8–14), but unlikely in most cases.[45] The account shares some similarities with the Wisdom of Solomon 12:3–11, pronouncing divine judgment on the Canaanites for their idolatry.[46]

God's judgment is pronounced by the prophets on the nations for their pride and arrogance. YHWH will "punish the arrogant boasting of the king of Assyria and his haughty pride" (Isa 10:12; cf. 37:36-38). An unnamed king of Babylon is denounced for his insolent onslaught (Heb. *marhēbâ* מַרְהֵבָה, Isa 14:4ff). A spirit of confusion (Heb. *ʿiwʿîm* עִוְעִים) is also pronounced on the Egypt of Isaiah's time (e.g., Isa 19:14). All of Israel's neighbors will be drunk with the cup of God's wrath (Jer 25:15-16). It all affirms YHWH's sovereignty over the world.[47]

The Hardening of the Israelites

"For the LORD had said to Moses, 'Say to the Israelites, "You are a stiff-necked people (*am-qəshēh-ʿōrep* עַם־קְשֵׁה־עֹרֶף)"'" (Exod 33:5; cf Acts 7:51a; LXX Exod 33:5).

---

44. On DtrH (Deuteronomy, Joshua, Judges, Samuel, Kings), see Noth, *Deuteronomistic History*, and Fretheim, *Deuteronomic History*.

45. In his novella, underscoring the difficulties people have with change, *Great Divorce*, Lewis has most of his characters from hellish Grey Town choose to *return* there, because of the challenges faced at the foothills of heaven (this "release time" from hell is called a *refrigerium*, 67).

46. In Wis 12:3-18. There is a clear intent to justify the Israelite conquest of Canaan. In Jewish-Hellenistic apologetics, this contention is inferred also from Jubilees 8:8-11; 9:14-15; 10:29-34. See Winston, *Wisdom of Solomon*, 238. .

47. On prophecies concerning the nations, see Isa 13-23; Jer 46-51; Ezek 25-32; Amos 1:3—2:16; and Zeph 2:4-15. Individual examples appear in Isaiah 34; Obadiah; Nahum, Sweeney, *Isaiah*, 213-14. See also Christensen, " Nations," 4:1037-49

This indictment of Israel was given after God's interaction with Moses regarding Israel's future in the aftermath of the golden calf debacle (Exod 32). God had delivered the people of Israel from Egypt (12–15) and had provided them with the Sinai covenant establishing them as YHWH's people (20–24).[48] Even in the covenant code, the people are reminded: "You shall take no bribe, for a bribe blinds (*'āwar* עִוֵּר)[49] the officials, and subverts the cause of those who are in the right" (Exod 23:8). In the final words of Moses (Deut 31:27), the people are still characterized as rebellious (*mərî*) and stiff-necked (*qāshe-ōrep*).

Much of the judgment threats of the prophets were influenced by the curses and threats of the ancient Israelites' covenant treaties.[50] These covenant threats were often directed to individual offenders of the covenant community (e.g., Nathan to David, Elijah to Ahab). It was the pre-exilic prophets of Amos and Isaiah who once again (as in Exodus and Deuteronomy) apply judgment to *all* Israel.[51] For the pre-exilic prophets, it was the foolish policies related to the Assyrian threat (eighth century) that prompted the hardening terminology being applied to all Israel, because the king and the people did not recognize their doom until it was too late, in the north 722 BCE and in the south 701 BCE (Amos 5:1–3; 8:1–3; Isa 10:5). Both prophets show Assyria to be an instrument of YHWH's judgment.

The desired response expected of God's people by its prophets was an obedient response to the divine word and deed.

> Exodus 4:11 (cf. Prov 20:12) summarizes the main doctrine underlying the thematic hardness of heart. God is the source of the

---

48. Fretheim, *Exodus*, 292. Exodus 33 appears to reflect a JE pre-exilic source.

49. Here and in Deuteronomy 16:19, Piel Imperfect, 3rd person singular. Heb. *āwar* is used also of physical blindness (2 Kgs 25:7; Jer 39:7/52:11), *HALOT*, 802. See also (*sanwērîm* סַנְוֵרִים) "dazzling, deception" (Gen 19:11; 2 Kgs 6:18), giving the physical blindness here, symbolic significance (see 2 Kgs 6:20, *HALOT*, 760–61). See also the less frequent *shā'a'* שָׁעַע used in the hiphil IMV in Isa 6:10, "be sealed over, besmeared"; hithpalel IMV in Isa 29:9a. "Behave as one's eyes are though blind," and the Qal IMV in Isa 29:9b, "be sealed tight, pasted over," HALOT 1612–13; GKC §67v. "We grope like the blind (*'iwwēr* עִוֵּר) along a wall," (Isa 59:10).

50. Routledge, "Blessings and Curses," 61–67. See also speech-act theory concerning the performative force of certain utterances in *Thiselton on Hermeneutics*, 61–66, 84–86, citing the works of, e.g., Austin, *Things with Words* and Searle, *Speech Acts*.

51. It is interesting to notice that DtrH seems to focus on individual offenders of God's covenant that is given to *all* Israel in Exodus and Deuteronomy. Often these individual offenders are kings who are supposed to represent the people. On corporate personality in ancient Israel, see my note ch. I, n54.

hearing ear and seeing eye. These two faculties function at their best when God's words and mighty acts are properly contemplated.[52]

Isaiah of Jerusalem (eighth century BCE with some later redactions)

The classic statement of hardening occurs in Isaiah 6:9-10. It is a commission directive that follows a vision report (vv. 1-8) of a theophany that includes an invitation ("whom shall I send?") and the prophet's reply ("send me"). It concludes (vv. 11-13) with the prophet's query ("how long?") and YHWH's reply (until judgment is complete). Isaiah 6:1-13 functions as the conclusion to previous chapters (2-5) and serves as an introduction to a memorial (*Denkschrift* "memoir") extending to 8:18.[53]

In his commission, the prophet is told that the results of his preaching would only increase the hardness of the people (and their leaders). It is "a hardened message for a calloused audience."[54]

COMMISSION REPORT OF ISAIAH 6:9-10[55]

1. Speech formula: "Go and say to this people" v. 9a

---

52. Danker, "Hardness of Heart," 89.

53. Otto Kaiser, *Isaiah 1-12* (1983), 119-20; Sweeney, *Isaiah 1-39* (1996), 135, eighth century material. The LXX of Isa 6:9-10, has less divine causation, for the people are inclined to harden their own heart. See Stenmans, "כָּבֵד κτλ," 21 (13-22). Later, I will show how the judgment and hardening statements are interrelated.

54. Quote from Smith, *Isaiah 1-39*, 88. (a) Sweeney sees a cultic setting for Isaiah 6 on Yom Kippur (742 BCE, Isa 6:1), when atonement is made for the people's sins (Lev 16:30-34), *Isaiah 1-39* (1996), 140. The prophet Isaiah must have participated in temple worship because he had closely observed its many abuses (Isa 1:11-16). (b) On the close interrelationship of the people and the king (cf. Isa 7:2, 17; 2 Kgs 23:3), see Robinson, *Corporate Personality*, 1-20. (c) Kaplan suggests that the life setting of Isaiah 6 reflects the prophet's despairing reflection on the failure of his attempts to convince the people to repent, written *after* he had been active for some time, in his "Isaiah 6:1-11," 251-59. (d) The literary function of Isaiah 6 as introduction to a memoir, reflects later redactional activity, composed shortly after the prophet's ministry, Kaiser, *Isaiah 1-12*, 119-20. Isaiah 6:11-13 appears to be an allusion to the Assyrian invasion (701 BCE). See also Kellenberger, "Heil und Verstockung"; Torsten, *Hardening in the Book of Isaiah*.

55. Outline derived from Sweeney, *Isaiah*, 132. On Isaiah 6 as a commission report (cf. 1 Kgs 22:19-23; Zech 1:7-17), rather than a call narrative, see Steck, "Jesaja 6," 188-206. As a call narrative, Isaiah 6 is *atypical* because of its similarities to 1 Kings

2. Content of what to say: "keep hearing but do not understand..." v. 9

3. Effect of commission on the people: "Make the heart of this people fat ..." v. 10a

4. Purpose of commission: "lest (conj., *pen* פֶּן) it may not look with its eyes..." v. 10b[56]

The message of the commission that results in hardening may concern the dangers of making foreign alliances, whether they be alliances against or with the powerful Assyrians (ch. 7).[57] Marvin Sweeney views Isaiah 6:1-11 as addressed to both Israel and Judah, as in 5:7, and relates to the approaching Assyrian threat. Whereas vv. 12-13 are addressed specifically to Judah, perhaps the Assyrian invasions (722-701 BCE).[58]

The response of hardening to Isaiah's message involves the faculties of perception and response (eyes, ears, and heart).[59] This type of saying may very well have been proverbial, as seen in Demosthenes, *Contra Aristogenes* 1: "so that the proverb results, 'Seeing they do not see, hearing they do not

---

22:19-23, see also Wildberger, *Isaiah 1-12*, 252. The prophet Amos, already established in his prophetic vocation, receives a similar commissioning vision (Amos 9:1-6), see Evans, *To See and Not Perceive*, 22.

56. Although a plurality is implied (e.g., NRSV), I favor the ET by Roberts that focuses on the culpability of the nation as a whole ("it" rather than "they" in v. 10): "Go and say to this people, 'Keep listening, but do not understand. Keep looking, but do not perceive.' Fatten the mind [heart] of this people, and its ears make heavy, and its eyes smear over, lest it should see with its eyes, and with its ears hear, and its [heart] should understand, and it turn and there be healing for it." Roberts, *First Isaiah*, 89, [brackets] mine. LXX has 3rd person pl. aor. indic. (*kammyō* καμμύω) and 3rd pl. subj. verbs in Isa 6:10 (e.g., ἴδωσιν *idōsin*) with pl. possessives ("their') and 1QIsaᵃ has *yeshāmû* ישמעו 3rd person pl. both lending support to the NRSV translation, e.g., of the Qal impf 3ms *yirʾeh* יִרְאֶה "lest *they* may not look" the Heb. verb 3rd sing. referring back to "this people" (noun common sing., *ʿam* עַם) v. 9, e.g., "this people, they...."

57. See also the hardening statement in Isaiah 29:10 with regard to the prophets/seers not recognizing Assyria as an instrument of YHWH's judgment. On the close interrelationship of the people with the king (and his court), see my ch. I, n54.

58. Sweeney, *Isaiah*, 138-39.

59. Oswalt notes the chiastic arrangement: A *heart*, B *ears*, C *eyes*, B' *ears*, A' *heart*, and comments that a "fat heart" (or "dull," Heb. שָׁמֵן *shāmēn*) speaks of a slow, languid, self-oriented set of responses, incapable of decisive, self-sacrificial action, *Isaiah 1-39*, 189n10. Hebrew שָׁמֵן *shāmēn* (Hiphil IMV) in Isa 6:10, used negatively here (see also 1QIsaᵃ) and in Ezek 34:16 (MT; cf. LXX), is used also of the "fatted calves" (1 Sam 15:9) and productive land (Neh 9:25, 35). See also that the heart is "unfeeling" (טָפַשׁ *tapash*) like "fat" (*ḥēleb* חֵלֶב) Ps 119:70, denoting insensitivity. The heart is also "deceitful" (*ʿāqōb* עָקֹב) Jer 17:10, and its "intentions" (*yētser* יֵצֶר) are (often) evil, Gen 8:21b.

hear.'" A similar proverb is found in Aeschylus, *Prometheus Bound* § 446: "Seeing, they saw in vain; and hearing, they did not understand."[60]

The Qur'an (7th cent. CE), Sūrat al-Baqara (the Cow) 2.7 addresses unbelievers "Allah has set a seal upon their hearts and upon their hearing and there is a covering over their eyes and there is a great punishment for them." In Q 2.10 for those who desire to deceive Allah "there is disease in their hearts, so Allah added to their disease and they shall have a painful chastisement." In Q 2.17–18, concerning those who follow error: "Allah took away their light, and left them in utter darkness—they do not see. Deaf, dumb, (and) blind, so they will not turn back."[61]

YHWH's hardening of the people and their leaders in Isaiah 6 has similarities with the account of Micaiah's commission in 1 Kings 22:19–23. As the "spirit" is to delude King Ahab (1 Kgs 22:20), Isaiah is to "harden" the people of Judah (and their leaders).[62] The resolute actions of the Israelite king (Ahab) waging war against the Arameans has parallels with the Pharaoh of Exodus: both stubbornly follow their own advisors against God's prophet and God responds by hardening them in their obstinacy. Perhaps the unjust actions of Isaiah's audience (Isa 5:18–23) have prompted this hardening statement of YHWH in Isaiah 6:9–10. The leaders of Israel and Judah are "drunk" with their dead-end policies (Israel, 28:7–8, 18; Judah, 30:1–3), so YHWH has poured a "spirit of stupor" (*tardēmâ* תַּרְדֵּמָה) and has "closed" (Piel of *ʿātsōm* עָצַם) the eyes" of the court prophets and royal counselors (Judah, 29:9–10).[63]

---

60. Quotations from Evans, *To See and Not Perceive*, 18. See fourth century BCE: Demosthenes, *Against Aristocrates*; fifth century BCE: Aeschylus, *Prometheus Bound*. On "seeing" and "not seeing," "knowing and "not knowing" in ancient drama, see also Seale, *Vision and Stagecraft*.

61. ET from *Qur'an* 1–2. Surah 2.8–19 are addressed to hypocritical or misled followers of Allah, see Pickthall, *Koran*, 34n2.

62. For further comparison of the two commissioning narratives, see Wildberger, *Isaiah 1–12*, 252; Sweeney, *Isaiah*, 134–35. "This people" blindly followed their leaders to trust in foreign alliances and thus reject the teaching of the prophet Isaiah, see my ch. I, n54.

63. Roberts, *First Isaiah*, 367–68. A similar pronouncement is made against Egypt of Isaiah's time, e.g., Isa 19:14. Paul will quote the LXX version in Rom 11:8 to discuss the hardening of Israel allowing for his gentile mission. See also the prophet's mission in the Hermetica (second–third centuries CE): "O peoples, earth-bound men, who have given yourselves up to drunkenness and sleep and to ignorance of God, be sober, cease your orgies, bewitched as you are by irrational sleep." Gk. text from Reitzenstein, *Poimandres*, ch. I §27.7–9 (p. 337). ET from Barrett, *NT Background*, 99.

The behaviors of the kings and the people are similar to that of ideologues: an "often blindly partisan advocate or adherent of a particular ideology."[64] They rarely listen to reasoned argument and facts, contrary to their views. They are hard-headed as well as hard-hearted. They will keep their ideology (e.g., foreign treaties, idolatry, exploitation) even if it may kill them or others (e.g., conquest, exile) because they already have invested too much in it.

> Blindness is used as the major image for ignorance of God (Is 6:9–10; 26:11; 29:9, 18; 35:5; 42:7, 16, 18–19; 43:8; 56:10). Zion's blindness is demonstrated in three ways: injustice (i.e., ill treatment of widows, orphans and poor [Is 1:17, 21]), foreign alliances (Is 31:1) and idolatry (Is 1:29–30).[65]

This hardening of the people is YHWH's judgment upon them for their disobedience: not heeding God's prophets, nor behaving as God's people.[66] "For they are a rebellious [*merî* מְרִי] people, deceitful [*keḥāsh* כֶּחָשׁ] sons, sons who are not willing to heed the torah of YHWH" (Isa 30:9, AT). It is in this judgment of hardening that the presence of YHWH is made known (Isa 6:9–10; 8:17). The hardening is to ripen the people for judgment, resulting in a surviving remnant (6:12–13; cf. Amos 5:3; 6:9).[67] After a certain point, however, the hardening judgment seems to be final (9:13–21). The hardening statement is a sovereign pronouncement of YHWH upon the people for

---

64. "Ideologues," in *Merriam-Webster*, 616.

65. Ryken, *Biblical Imagery*, 428. Physical blinding as punishment for wrongdoing was practiced by hostile nations (2 Kgs 25:7; Jer 39:7/52:11), but rarely in Israel. To accomplish his divine purpose, God (or angel, prophet) will temporarily blind individuals or groups (Gen 19:11; 2 Kgs 6:18; Acts 9:8–9; 13:11). Jesus refuted the prevalent idea that physical blindness was evidence of divine punishment (John 9:1–3; cf. Luke 13:2–3; Exod 20:5). Figurative blindness refers to the inability to recognize the truth, whether it is injustice (Deut 16:19; Isa 1:21–23; Job 9:24), idolatry (Isa 44:9–10), bad policies (30:1–7), or failure to understand (e.g., Isa 43:8). Ibid., 99.

66. "Yet the peoples saw and did not understand, nor take such a thing to heart" (Wis 4:15). Charles makes this connection with Isa 6:9–10 in his *Apocrypha*, 1:541.

67. See Kellenberger, "Heil und Verstockung." Although it is retained in 1QIsa[a] the phrase, "holy seed" is *not* found in LXX, but a remnant idea is still conveyed "those who have been left . . . a tenth" (NETS, 830). Judgment is often viewed as a purifying process that involves purging evil from Israel and producing a remnant (Is 1:25–26; 6:11–13; 10:20–23; "purify," *bārar* בָּרַר Ezek 20:38). On Judah as a remnant after Assyrian invasion (Isa 6:12–13), see Sweeney, *Isaiah*, 138.

their sins. Such a pronouncement has a "performative function" utilized by the OT prophets and the NT evangelists (cf. Acts 28:26–28).[68]

What appears to be a later redaction, the promise of restoration is given: "strengthen (*ḥāzaq*) weak hands, make firm (*ametz*) feeble knees, to the fearful be strong (*ḥāzaq*);[69] . . . the eyes of the blind shall be opened, and the ears of the deaf unstopped" (Isa 35:3–5; cf. 30:20–21; 32:3–4; 41:20; 61:1).

> **And the eyes of them that see shall not be closed, and the ears of them that hear shall attend** [Isa 32:3]. In other words, the need in their regard was that they should have **eyes to see** [Deut 29:3]—that they should **see and receive instruction** [Prov 24:32] **and ears to hear** [Deut 29:3] . . . **to observe and to do** [Deut 28:3] according to all that might be commanded them.[70]

Jeremiah (sixth century BCE)[71]

As we saw in Isaiah of Jerusalem, Jeremiah uses similar hardening terminology, for example, in Jeremiah 5:20–31: " a foolish and heartless people" (v. 21 *'am sākāl wəʾēn lēb* עַם סָכָל וְאֵין לֵב), this people have a "foolish and stubborn heart" (v. 23 *lēb sōrēr ûmôreh* לֵב סוֹרֵר וּמוֹרֶה; cf., Isa. 6:9–10; blind, deaf, 43:8; "a house of rebels" *bēyt-hammerî* בֵּית־הַמֶּרִי, blind, deaf, Ezek 12:2) but here the people's spiritual blindness (eyes that do not see) and deafness (ears that do not hear) are due to persuasive false prophets, *not* the prophets of YHWH (Jer 5:21 with 5:31).[72] In addition, the people "will not listen" because of false worship (Jer 7:27 and 7:32). Hardening in Jeremiah is often a prerequisite to judgment (e.g., from Babylon), *not* judgment itself.

---

68. See my ch. I, n50 on speech-act theory.

69. Notice how the hardening language is used in a positive sense: "strengthen (*ḥāzaq*) weak hands, make firm (*ametz*) feeble knees, to the fearful be strong (*ḥāzaq*). See *HALOT*, 65, 302–303. See also Harmon, *Rebels and Exiles*, 89, 135.

70. Quotation from a fifteenth-century treatise on the rhetoric of the Hebrew Bible by Leon, *Honeycomb's Flow*, 519. Bold print is in original quotation.

71. On the two divergent texts of Jeremiah (lengthier MT and shorter LXX), see Goldingay, *Jeremiah*, 43–45. On the book's "elaborate tapestry of meaning-making that honors complexity, delights in ambiguity," see his pp. 60–61.

72. Goldingay, *Jeremiah*, 203–5. In the eighth century *Mandaean Prayerbook*, 133, the Messenger/emissary from above addresses *Ruha*, an evil spirit: "your eyes are eyes of lying . . . the eyes of lying grow dark and do not see the truth." ET from Puskas and Robbins, *Conceptual Worlds*, 163.

All Israel will be judged (586 BCE) but a remnant will survive.[73] Unlike Isaiah, Jeremiah is reluctant to connect the hardening of the people with the acts of YHWH. God's call to return is extended (18:11), but "everyone walks after his stubborn, evil heart" (AT; "stubborn," *sherirut*, Jer 7:24; 16:12; 18:12). In Jeremiah 5:3-5 (and Hos 4:16), the image derives from cattle used as draft animals, whose power seems to be concentrated in the neck.[74] Whoever resists the yoke is "hard-necked."[75] See also Jeremiah 17:9, "The heart is deceitful (*lēb 'aqôb*; לֵב עָקֹב)[76] above all things." Jeremiah gives more room for free will in the hardening process: "Circumcise yourselves to YHWH and remove the foreskins of your heart" (4:4; cf. Deut 10:16).[77]

Second and Third Isaiah (sixth century BCE)

In Second Isaiah of Babylon, sixth century BCE, we observe that hardening is a necessity for both Israel and the Servant in order that deliverance may occur (Isa 42:18-20; 43:8).[78] YHWH has not abandoned Israel. Israel is in exile because of her sins (48:4, 8). Nevertheless, YHWH offers hope of salvation to those who are "blind" and "deaf" (42:18-20; 43:8-11). Those who make idols for their worship in Babylon are hardened (44:9, 18),[79] but there is hope for a new exodus to the promised land (44:21-28).

---

73. See Jeremiah 27:1—28:17, under the yoke of Babylon, but hope is given to the faithful in exile (29:10-14). In 2 Esdras 3:20-27, an evil heart was in Adam to disobey and this burden *continued* in his descendants who were given the law, it is why Jerusalem was delivered into the hands of the Babylonians (vv. 27-28).

74. For more on this draft animal image, see my ch. I, n11. Also, LXX Jer 5:3 uses στερεόω *stereō* "they made their faces hard." It is often used in a more positive sense: Isa 50:7 "set my face like a rock"; adj. στερεός *stereos* "firm in faith," 1 Pet 5:9.

75. קשה *qšh* "to be hard" by van der Woude 3:1176.

76. A heart that is "insidious, deceitful," related to the verb *āqab* עָקַב "to circumvent, overreach," the deceptive actions of Jacob with Esau (Gen 25:26; 27:36). See also "crooked, perverted heart," LXX *kardia steblē*, καρδία στρεβλή; cf. LXX Sir 36:20 (Sir numbering follow, *Septuaginta*).

77. See Jer 7:31-32; 19:4-5; 44:4-5; cf. Deut 30:15-20; Isa 66:3-4; Eccl 7:29 cited by Meadors in support of free will, *Hardening of the Heart*, 189, although a propensity for choosing the wrong way is especially evident in the above verses (e.g., the debate using Scripture in Luther's *Bondage of the Will*).

78. Baltzer discusses the irony of Israel as a blind servant and deaf messenger, in his *Deutero-Isaiah*, 149-50, 163. On how First Isaiah gets reworked later in canonical Isaiah, see Sommer, *Prophet Reads Scripture*. Torsten demonstrates this reworking in his synchronic study *Hardening in the Book of Isaiah*.

79. Meadors examines the biblical rationale for idolatry and the hardening of the

In Third Isaiah we observe that the hardening of the people is an expression and a result of YHWH's wrath (57:17–18; 63:17; cf. Deut 29:18; Jer 8:5).[80] Here YHWH "hands over" the hardened to their sin (Isa 64:7; cf. Hos 11:8; Gk. *paradidōmi*, Rom 1:24, 26, 28). To avert the hardening one must cry out to or plead with YHWH for deliverance: "Lord, why have you allowed us to turn from your path? Why have you given us stubborn hearts so we no longer fear you?" (Isa 63:17 NLT).[81]

On "hand over/deliver" in Isaiah 64:7, the *NET Bible* translates it literally as "and you caused us to melt in the hand of sin," but emends it to read "and you handed us over." The point is that God has abandoned them to their sinful ways and no longer seeks reconciliation.[82]

We see that it is Israel's sentinels/watchers (cf. blind, mute, Isa 56:10; Ezek 33:6) and shepherds (Ezek 34:2–4; Zech 11:3–5) who are the special center of God's wrath and hardening activity (Isa 56:10–11). Life away from YHWH is hardening connected with sin, something to which YHWH will give them over (Isa 57:13a, 20–21).

Ezekiel (sixth century, BCE)

Like Isaiah of Jerusalem, Ezekiel has the hardening terms in the account of his commission, but for him they seem to be forms of the prophet's call (cf. Isa 6:9–10; 1 Kgs 22).[83] The prophet sees a vision, is called by YHWH,

---

heart as it unfolds in specific passages—Lev 26, Deut 29, Pss 115, 135—and examines the phenomenon through the rest of the Hebrew Bible, the Gospels, the letters of Paul, and Revelation, in his *Hardening of the Heart*. See also Lints, *Identity and Idolatry*, 93–94.

80. Hebrew scholar, Paul, sees some hope of healing in Isa 57:19, but not for the wicked, vv. 20–21, *Isaiah 40–66*, 478.

81. Tigay has argued for this tolerative Hiphil of "to wander, stray," *tā'a* תָּעָה (adopted only in NLT) in "Tolerative/Permissive Hiphil," 411. Tigay has also cited in support Eichrodt, *Theology of the OT* 2:178, on human responsibility for sin and the divine will. On tolerative Hiphil, see my discussion in ch. I, n33.

82. The verb וַתְּמוּגֵנוּ (*watəmûgēnû*) is a Qal preterite 2nd person masculine singular with a 1st person common plural suffix from the root מוג (*mûg*, "melt"). However, elsewhere the Qal of this verb is intransitive. If the verbal root מוג (*mûg*) is retained here, the form should be emended to a Polel pattern (וַתְּמֹגְגֵנוּ, *watəmōgəgēnû*). The translation assumes an emendation to וַתְּמַגְּנֵנוּ (*watəmagənēnû*, "and you handed us over"). This form is a Piel preterite 2nd person masculine singular with a 1st person common plural suffix from the verbal root מגן (*miggēn*, "hand over, surrender"); see *HALOT* 545 s.v. מגן and BDB 171 s.v. מָגַן), *NET Bible* (2007), 1372. See also Paul, *Isaiah 40–66*, 586.

83. On Ezekiel, I consulted Zimmerli, *Ezekiel 1*, 100–107. On the literary style of

and encounters nations of rebels (*mārâ* מָרָה), a people who are "stiff-faced" (*qəshê-pānîm* קְשֵׁי פָנִים), and hardened (*ḥāzaq* חָזָק, Ezek 2:3–4; 3:7–9; cf. 1QS 5:5). The hardening by YHWH is mentioned to underscore the guilt of the people: they have failed to see the disaster of Judah as YHWH's judgment upon them for their sins. Ezekiel 12:2 (e.g., a rebellious house with eyes that do not see, and ears that do not hear), recalls similar language as Isaiah 6:9–10 with related parallels (Deut 29:3; Jer 5:21; Pss 115:5–7; 135:16–17; Mark 4:12; 8:18). The hardening language in Psalms 115:4–8 and 135:15–18, also reflecting that of Isaiah 6:9–10, are used for the mocking of idols: e.g., they have eyes, but do not see, ears, but do not see.[84] Perhaps Ezekiel confronts a people who are as unresponsive as the foreign idols they so revere.[85] Here as before it is merely hardening dogma, describing the hardened state of the people that Ezekiel has been called to address. It is a judgment of hardening, but it is *not final*. YHWH will give the people a new heart, not a heart of stone, but a heart of flesh (Heb. *lēb bāsār* לֵב בָּשָׂר 11:19; 36:26).[86]

Deuteronomy and Deuteronomistic History (sixth century BCE, and earlier)

The phrase *'āmētz-lēb* (אָמֵץ־לֵב) applied earlier to the non-Israelite Sihon (Deut 2:30) is now applied to the people of Israel. Moses warns his fellow Israelites not to be hardhearted (*'āmētz-lēb*)[87] and fail to provide for the needs of the poor among them (15:7) or accept bribes that "blind (*'āwar* עָוֵר)[88] the eyes of the wise" (Deut 16:19). Miroslav Volf stated it well:

Ezekiel, see Block, *Ezekiel 1–24*, 23–26.

84. Meadors views Pss 115 and 135 as key texts in his *Hardening of the Heart*, 2, 49.

85. Zimmerli, *Ezekiel 1*, 270. Foreign attendants may also have been serving in the temple, those identified as *'erel lēb wə'erel bāsār* עֲרֵל לֵב וְעֲרֵל בָּשָׂר "uncircumcised of heart and uncircumcised flesh" (Ezek 44:7, 9), see Block, *Ezekiel 2*:622–23.

86. In the NT, Gk. *kardian sarkinēn* καρδίαν σαρκίνην can occur in positive, see 2 Cor 3:3; cf. LXX Ezek 11:19; 36:26, neutral (human descent, Heb 7:16), and negative senses (in contrast to *pneumatikos* πνευματικός, 1 Cor 3:1; Rom 7:14), see BDAG, 914.

87. Steinmann, "Hardness of Heart," 381. Craigie, *Deuteronomy*, 237–238.

88. Here as in Exod 23:8, Piel Imperfect, 3rd person singular of *āwar*: "a bribe blinds," a proverbial saying. Used also of physical blindness (2 Kgs 25:7; Jer 39:7/52:11), *HALOT*, 802. See my ch. I, n65. See also (*sanwērîm* סַנְוֵרִים) "dazzling, deception," Gen 19:11; 2 Kgs 6:18, giving the physical blindness here, symbolic significance, see 2 Kgs 6:20.

How can the exodus from the "house of slavery" into the promised land take place when Pharaoh's horses and chariots are on *both sides* of the Red Sea? Indeed, how can it take place when we ourselves are Pharaohs ruling in the land of exclusion, from which we should be liberated?[89]

I observe also some parallels to Isaiah 6:9-10 in the historical prologue of a covenant renewal ceremony of Israel (Deut 29:2-29). Although it does reflect the ancient treaty form and provides some evidence for such a ceremony appearing early in Israel's history, the recital contains some post-exilic redaction (e.g., Deut 29:28, people uprooted from their land), perhaps it is a later addition by DtrH (Deuteronomistic Historian) to the Deuteronomic code. Here the people have no perceptive heart, eyes, and ears to respond to the acts of God (v. 4 [ET]; cited in Rom 11:8 along with Isa 29:10; LXX Deut 29:3).[90] Some have already begun to follow the detestable idols of the nations (29:18), thinking that they are safe in their stubborn שְׁרִירוּת (*shərîrût*) ways (29:18 MT; cf. Jer 3:17; Ps 81:13).[91]

Although the people are to remember their history from this divine perspective, they are beset by anxieties and temptations, and so "there is a continual return to the theme in the address of Moses, in order that the audience might be brought to real understanding of the ways of God, real seeing of the acts of God, and real hearing of the words of God."[92] In the concluding speech of Moses: "For I know how rebellious (מְרִי *marî*) and stubborn (קָשֶׁה *qāsheh*) you are. Behold, even today while I am yet alive

---

89. Volf, *Exclusion and Embrace*, 92. The rebellion even has a longer history: "You have been rebellious (Hiphil of *mārâ* מָרָה) against the Lord as long as I have known you," Deut 9:24 MT. See also " I spread out my hands all day to a rebellious (*sārar* סָרָר) people" Isa 65:2.

90. "The LORD has not given you a heart to know, eyes to see, and ears to hear up to this day," is located at Deut 29:3 in LXX, MT, Vulgate, and 4Q39 on Deut 29:3. The discrepancy is because Deut 29:1 (ET) is 28:69 in MT to close out the future blessings and curses of Deut 27-28, see Rad, *Deuteronomy*, 178.

91. In 1 Kgs 15:13 (DtrH), King Asa of Judah cut down a "detestable image" מִפְלֶצֶת (*mipletset*) of Ashera, in the Latin Vulgate *confregit simulacrum turpissimum* ("he broke the effigy most disgraceful"), *simulacrum* also denotes a "false image or copy" (Gk. *pseudēs mimēmata*, Plato, *Sophist* 240, 264). The idol worshipper shares the inanimate and inauthentic characteristics of the idol that is worshipped (Deut 29:4, 17-19; cf. Ps 115:4-8; Jer 51:17-18).

92. Craigie, *Deuteronomy*, 356. Moses will also challenge the people to "circumcise the foreskin of their hearts" (Deut 10:16; 30:6 *mûl* מוּל Qal perf.), used also in Jer 4:4 (*mûl* Nifal). Similar metaphorical language is used in the opening invective of the Stephen speech ("you ... uncircumcised of heart and ears" Acts 7:51) relying on the LXX.

with you, you have been rebellious against the LORD" (Deut 31:27). Although linked as a conclusion to the blessings and curses of the covenant (27–28), it fits in well with DtrH retribution doctrine: rebellion brings God's wrath; repentance brings God's mercy.

In chapter 32 we have another DtrH addition of a covenant renewal festival. Here the history of Israel as a rebellious people is recited ("Jeshurun [Jacob/Israel] grew fat" *shāmēn* שָׁמֵן. . . . abandoned God" v.15; on first Heb. verb here, see n59).

Although this text again reflects an ancient treaty form, allusions to the exile (586 BCE) place it at a later date (Deut 32:17, 39), and DtrH concepts in Deut 32:15–17 seem similar to Second Isaiah (40:19–20). It was more characteristic of the exilic and post-exilic periods that the people were profoundly aware of their *collective* guilt and sin and saw this condition in retrospect to their *entire* history. We will see this recital in a more complete form in the post-exilic ceremony of Nehemiah 9. In the above examples, the condition of the people as hardened to God's benevolent acts is underscored.

All of these accounts reflect the retribution doctrine of DtrH: the people have done wrong so they are punished by YHWH. If they do good they will be blessed. This doctrine is especially seen in the accounts of individuals whose tragic downfall is explained as being hardened by YHWH. God takes action against Abimelech for eliminating all potential rivals to the throne of Shechem (Judg 9:23). Eli's sons are killed because they sinned against the Lord (1 Sam 2:25). The Lord has taken the kingdom from Saul and given it to David (1 Sam 18:6–11; 19:9–11; 24:16–17; 28:15–19; 31:1–7).[93] When the character of these men becomes wicked and sinful, God intervenes with his hardening activity (sending an evil spirit to Saul, 18:10; 19:9) to bring about their punishment. Even the (non-Israelite) Philistines remind themselves of this fate when they had captured the ark (1 Sam 6:6) using *kābēd* (כָּבֵד) to recall the self-hardening of Pharaoh and the Egyptians: "Why should you harden your hearts as the Egyptians and Pharaoh hardened their hearts?" The Dtr Historian wants his audience to know that even the Philistines fear Israel's God who rewards the righteous and punishes the disobedient (see my n43, on Sihon).

---

93. The following works connect the fall of the houses of Saul (Mephibosheth) and David (Zedekiah) with blind and death disabilities and their symbolic meanings in the narrative, Ceresko, "'The Blind' and 'Lame,'" 23–30, and Schipper, "Disability," 422–34.

In 1 Kings 22:1–38, discussed earlier, the resolute actions of the Israelite king (Ahab) who chooses to wage war against the Arameans has parallels with the Pharaoh of Exodus: both stubbornly follow their own advisors against God's prophet and God responds by hardening them in their obstinacy.[94] God's sending a lying spirit into the mouths of the king's court prophets merely supports the king's resolute action to attack Ramoth-gilead under the king of Aram, which end in the king of Israel's death (fulfilling Elijah's earlier prophecy, 1 Kgs 21:19).

Walter Brueggemann, commenting on this episode:

> It is astonishing but regularly the case that human power succumbs to arrogance and hubris that culminate in destruction. In our time the most dramatic cases, of course, are those of Adolf Hitler and Joseph Stalin.[95]

Wisdom and the Psalms (sixth century BCE, with earlier traditions)

Although there was some reservations about it in the books of Qoheleth (e.g., Eccl 8:14—9:4) and Job (e.g., Job 12:13–25; 25:4–6), the later Psalms and Wisdom Literature continue much of the retribution doctrine with many occurrences of the righteous being blessed and the sinful hardened.[96] The wicked represent "the proud (zēd זֵד), haughty (yāhîr יָהִיר) person" who "acts with arrogant pride"(zādôn זָדוֹן, Prov 21:24).

In Proverbs 28:14 we see that the man who fears God is blessed, and he who hardens (Hiphil participle of qāshâ קָשָׁה) his heart will fall into calamity. Bruce Waltke comments here

> When one hardens his heart his psyche can no longer feel, respond, and opt for a new direction. The hardened heart is fixed in unbelief and unbending defiance to God (Exod 7:3; Ps 95:8); insensible to admonition or reproof it cannot be moved to a new sphere of behavior.... [T]he trembling heart is one that is an open heart to God and responds to the prompting of his Spirit to redirect his life away from this hostility.[97]

---

94. See 2 Thess 2:9–11, where God sends followers of the lawless one a "power that deludes (*planē*) so that they believe what is false (*pseudos*)."

95. Brueggemann, *1 & 2 Kings*, 278. On hubris, see "ὕβρις," LSJ, 1841.

96. Walton, "Retribution," 647–55.

97. Waltke, *Proverbs*, 419. "The heart was one's emotional center in a positive or

Regarding Proverbs 29:1 "One who is reproved, yet stiffens the neck (*maqsheh 'ōrep*), will suddenly be broken beyond healing." Bruce V. Malchow includes it within Proverbs 28:28—29:2 as "the central structural verses in the collection." As the centerpiece, Proverbs 28:28—29:2 thus colors the entire section (Prov 28-29) with the danger of resisting wisdom's reproofs.[98]

In Psalm 69 is the imprecatory prayer of a righteous man that his adversaries be hardened: "let their eyes be darkened that they cannot see" (pl. possessives & verbs, v. 23; 69:24 MT).[99] Later, Paul cites this passage (Ps 68:23-24 LXX) in Romans 11:9-10 to support the hardening of Israel in his gentile mission.

Israel's rebellion in the wilderness (cf. Deut 9:23; Ps 106:13-33) is recalled with hardening language in Psalm 78:8 "stubborn and rebellious" (*sōrēr ûmōreh* סוֹרֵר וּמֹרֶה), and vv. 40, 56 "rebelled" (Hiphil of *mārâ* מָרָה). Recalling the wilderness rebellion with a phrase often used in Jeremiah (3:17; 7:24; 9:13), Psalm 81:13, I gave them over "to their stubborn hearts" (*bishrîrût libbām* בִּשְׁרִירוּת לִבָּם). The verb "I gave them over" (Piel of *shālaḥ* שָׁלַח) recalls Romans 1:24, 26 and a possible allusion to the LXX translation "I dismissed" them (Ps 80:13, aorist of *exapostellō* ἐξαποστέλλω). See also my discussion on Isaiah 64:7 "you have handed us over to our sins" (see my p. 24).

In the kingship psalm (Ps 95) the people are exhorted not to harden their hearts (v.8, *qāsheh lēb* קָשָׁה לֵב) as their rebellious ancestors did (vv. 7b-11; cf. hardening interpretation of the rebellion in Exod 17:1-7; Num 20:1-13). Gerstenberger comments

> At Massah and Meribah—thus the meaning of the names—Israel "tried" Yahweh and "quarreled" with him (cf. also v. 9). For him, however, this event was a "hardening of hearts" (v. 8a) comparable to Isaiah's message of "fattening of hearts" (Isa 6:10). The Dtr metaphor is frequently "hardening [or 'stiffening'] of necks" (cf. Deut 9:6, 13; 10:16; 31:27; 2 Kgs 17:14; Jer 7:26; 17:23; 19:15). Evaluation of the whole wilderness period (40 years, v. 10a) leads

---

negative sense depending on the character of the individual." Meadors, *Hardness of Heart*, 15. See Prov 28:14. See also my ch. I, n22.

98. Malchow, "Future Monarchs," 241. For an outline of the entire framework of Proverbs 28-29, see Waltke, *Proverbs*, 405. See Sir 30:8 where an "unchecked son" is compared to a "stubborn" (*sklēros*) unbroken horse.

99. Gerstenberger regards Ps 69:23 as the imprecation of an individual complaint (Ps 69) from the exilic or post-exilic period, *Psalms*, 49-50.

Yahweh to the conclusion that his people do not want to follow his directions (v. 10bc). Therefore he swears not to let them come "to my tranquility" or "rest" (v. 11).[100]

Hebrews 3:8, 15, and 4:7 will revisit Psalm 95 (Ps 94 LXX) and the hardening of Israel in the wilderness (that I will discuss in ch. II).

Chronicles-Ezra-Nehemiah (fifth century BCE)

Two phrases, *qāseh 'ōrep* (קָשֵׁה עֹרֶף) "stiff-neck" and *āmētz lēb* (אָמֵץ-לֵב) "hard heart" are applied to king Zedekiah who disobeyed the Lord and his prophet, Jeremiah (2 Chr 36:13).[101] As Ralph W. Klein observes

> The exile is blamed on the sins of Zedekiah and his generation (vv. 11–17), not on Manasseh, as in Kings (2 Kgs 21:10–16; 23:26–27; 24:3–4). Manasseh, after all, had repented in mid-career and prospered for the remainder of his reign. The Deuteronomistic evaluation of Jehoahaz in 2 Kgs 23:32 is also left out.[102]

Here also in a post-exilic setting of a covenant renewal ceremony, the acts of God are recited along with the hardening of Israel to bring out a confession of sins by the people before a righteous God (Neh 9:16–17, 26, 29).

The hortatory character of Nehemiah 9 is clear. The author felt his solidarity with the history of unfaithfulness of his forebears. He also felt the burden of sins of his own time weighing down on his people. True to their history the Jews repaid the mercy and good acts of the Lord with ingratitude on every occasion. After they were punished by the Lord, they would be faithful for a while, but as soon as they were prosperous, they

---

100. Gerstenberger, *Psalms*, 184. Gerstenberg regards Ps 95 as a YHWH kingship psalm reflecting post-exilic worship with hymnic material (3–5, 7ab), calls to worship (vv 1–2, 6) and a concluding homily (7c–11).

101. LXX has "he hardened his neck (*sklērunō trachēlos*) and held back his heart (*katiskuō kardia*) not to return to the Lord God." LXX 1 Esdras 1:46 on Zedekiah's disobedience "he hardened his neck (*sklērunō trachēlos*) and his heart (*kardia*)." See also on the neck, my ch. I, n11.

102. Klein, *2 Chronicles*, 535. Only 2 Kings 25:7 states that Zedekiah is physically blinded (by the Babylonians). Is there some connection between this physical disablement and the end of the Davidic house through misunderstanding and spiritual blindness? See the following work that cites examples in other literature between physical disability as a metaphor for social downfall, Mitchell and Snyder, *Narrative Prosthesis*, 47–48, cited by Schipper in support of this biblical theme, "Disability," 533–34.

became again unfaithful to the Lord. This is an ancient theme, familiar throughout the entire OT. The author has rediscovered a general truth that is real even today.[103]

There follows a similar pattern of liturgy reflected in the Qumran covenant renewal ceremony (1QS 1.24-25; CD 3.10-16a). It is only after the exile that the prophetic judgment speeches had a profound effect on the guilt of the people. Only those post-exilic ceremonies of covenant renewal (e.g., Neh 9) contain lengthy reminders of Israel's sins.

Second Esdras (IV Ezra in Lat. Vulgate), a late-first century CE text, was probably written by a Palestinian Jew (containing some Christian redactions). It is added here because it denounces those of Israel who disregard God's law (2 Esd 7:22-24). With the revelation of the Messiah, the remnant will enjoy life for a set period of time (vv. 26-30).[104]

Old Testament Summation

The hardening terminology is diverse, metaphorically applied to various parts of the body: the heart, ears, eyes, the face, the forehead, the neck, the shoulder, and the back. It is concerned with non-receptivity.

In Exodus 4-14, the contest is highlighted between God hardening Pharaoh and Pharaoh's own self hardening. The question of whose actions began the hardening is open ended, despite source-critical speculations from J or JE, and P (tenth to fifth centuries BCE). Narrative criticism underscores the contest where YHWH gets glory over Pharaoh, in a kind of holy war, as a witness to both Israel and Egypt. Some of these themes carry over into YHWH's other conflicts with non-Israelites, e.g., Sihon (Deut 2:30), Canaanite kings (Josh 11:20), and the nations (Jer 25:15-16), where arrogance and idolatry are grave concerns.

In Deuteronomic history (sixth century BCE and earlier), certain individuals (Abimelech, sons of Eli, Saul), become hardened, before the onslaught of the Assyrian threat when hardening pronouncements are made upon the king and the people. The language of hardening of Isaiah 6:9-10 had some influence on the later statements of this composite work

---

103. Fensham, *Ezra and Nehemiah*, 228-29. On the structure of the covenant renewal of Nehemiah 9:1—10:39, see Throntveit, *Ezra-Nehemiah*, 100-109.

104. Meyers, *I and II Esdras*, structural outline, 108-10, 2 Esdras 7 addressed to Israel, 122, on messiah, 127, date, 129. On the reception, genre, and interpretation of 2 Esdras, see also Humphrey, "Esdras, Second," 309-13.

(Isa 35:3–5; 42:18–20; 44:9; 56:10–11; 63:17), as well as in Jeremiah 5:20–31, and in Ezekiel 2:3–3:9; 12:2; 33:6. There is great concern about obeying false prophets (Jer 5:20, 31) and partaking in idolatry (Isa 44:9, 18; 48:4–5, 8), but after judgment, a remnant will emerge (Isa 6:13; 10:20–21; 11:11–12; 43:5–7).[105]

On the mocking of idols, Psalms 115:4–8 and 135:15–18 state their deaf and mute features in a prophetic manner (Isa 44:9, 18; all post-exilic). A hardening statement is also pronounced on the enemies of the righteous (Ps 69:23) and the people are warned not to harden their hearts as the ancestors had done (Ps 85; cf. Heb 3:8–4:7). Proverbs 29:1 (re. one who is stiff-necked after reproof) is part of Proverbs 28:28—29:2, considered to be the centerpiece of the collection. In the post-exilic 2 Chronicles 36:13, King Zedekiah (ca. 586 BCE) is called stiff-necked for disobeying the Lord. Does his physical blindness, inflicted by his Babylonian captors (2 Kgs 25:27), have a metaphorical connection with his own spiritual blindness (2 Chr 36:12–13)? In Nehemiah 9, the hardening of Israel is recited along with the merciful acts of God performed on Israel's behalf (late fifth century BCE). Second Esdras 7:22–24, centuries later, still echoes Nehemiah and Israel's prophets in denouncing those who would disregard God's law.

Concerning the hardness of heart motif in holy war ideology, so prominent in the Deuteronomic writings, we see this development:

> The holy war ideology was shared with Israel's neighbors, and war between them and Israel was a contest between their gods (e.g., 2 Kgs 3:21–27). The immediate postexilic prophets draw on the imagery and ideology of the divine warrior to describe God's intervention to bring about the ideal eschatological age (Isa 59:15b–20; 63:1–6; 63:19b–64:1 [Eng 64:1–3]; Zech 9:1–17; 10:1–12; 14:4).[106]

---

105. Those surviving the Assyrian invasion, Heb. *sheār*, Isaiah 10–11; but also remnant of Assyria, 10:19; returning from the Babylonian exile, Heb. *sheērith*, Isa 46:3–4; Jer 23:3; 31:7–8; Ezek 9:8; 11:13; cf. remnant of other nations, Amos 1:8; 9:12; *pelētah*, Ezra 9:8; gathering of diaspora, Isa 66:20–21; God will create a "righteous" remnant, Zeph 3:11–13; Mal 3:16–18; cf. Gk. *leimma*, Rom 11:5. See Conrad, "Remnant," 761–62; Meyer, "Remnant," 669–71.

106. Scullion, "God in OT," 1047.

II

New Testament[1]

As I STATED IN chapter I, the challenge for both synchronic and diachronic approaches is interpreting the hardening motif in its proper literary and historical contexts with special consideration given to its Hellenistic Jewish and Greco-Roman environments. I am familiar with the hasty comparisons and contrasts that have been made between Hebrew and Greek thought and the project of developing a theology from linguistic analysis alone with little attention to contextual study. The challenge is doing justice to a complex theme that stretches from the first two centuries of our common era, paying attention to different socio-cultural contexts along the way.[2]

Lexical Terms and Equivalents

In the NT we see several lexical terms and their equivalents, but the expressions are here more closely associated with LXX Isaiah 6:9–10 (and Exod 33:3, 5; Ps 95:7–11 [Ps 94:7b–11 LXX]).[3]

---

1. On NT canon, see Gamble, *Canon*; Collins et al., *Christian Scriptures*, esp. 97–44, and McDonald, "Canon," 536–47. Books outside the Catholic and Protestant twenty-seven-book canon (e.g., 1–2 Clement; Barnabas; Hermas) will be consulted as they relate to the theme of hardness of heart.

2. See my ch. I, n5 on works by James Barr highlighting these concerns. See also discussion in Anthony Thiselton "Semantics," 75–104.

3. Helpful works consulted in this section are: Gnilka, *Die Verstockung Israels*; Evans, *To See and Not Perceive*; Spicq and Ernest, *Theological Lexicon*; and *TDNT*. The

pōroō—πωρόω "make stubborn, harden," John 12:40 (noun *pārōsis*, πώρωσις)[4]

sklērynō—σκληρύνω "make stubborn, harden" (noun, *sklērotēs* σκληρότης); "hardness," *sklērotrachēlos* σκληροτράχηλος—"stiff-necked," Acts 7:51; LXX Exod 33:3; Sir 16:11; "hardness of heart" *sklērokardia* σκληροκαρδία, Mark 10:5; (16:14); Philo *Spec* 1:305

typhloō τυφλόω—"to blind" John 12:40; Philo *Ebr* 108 (noun, "blind," *typhlos*, τυφλός)

skotizō σκοτίζω," Rom 1:21; *skotoō*—σκοτόω "to darken" Eph 4:18; 1 Clem 36:2

also negative *mē* μή plus *oida* οἶδα ("know") and/or *syniēmi* συνίημι "comprehend, understand" (subjunctive modes), Mark 4:12

The hardening terminology, using *some* the Old Testament imagery (see my ch. I, Lexical Terms), respecting *different* contexts,[5] is metaphorically applied to various parts of the body: the heart (Eph 4:18; Heb 3:8), mind (Rom 1:28; Eph 4:17; Gk. *nous*),[6] the ears (deaf, failure to listen), the eyes (lack of perception, Mark 4:11–12), and the neck (resistance, Acts 7:51; LXX Exod 33:3, 5).[7] As in the Old Testament, hardness of heart here reflects both inability and refusal to understand.

---

anti-Semitic views of Kittel, ed., are disturbing, see discussion in my Appendix.

4. πωρόω "to cause someone to be completely unwilling to learn and to accept new information," Louw and Nida, *Lexicon*, 332. Regarding *pōrōsis*, πώρωσις, Nanos cites ancient medical texts to argue that the hardening (Rom 11:25) is "a protective callus" that can be "healed" over time, in his *Reading Romans*, 153–78. As I indicated in my ch. I, n59, the hardness of heart includes broad and diverse meanings as in, e.g., Isaiah 6:10 where "fat heart" (Heb. שָׁמֵן *shāmēn*) speaks of a slow, languid, set of responses, incapable of decisive action.

5. I am not implying here that the semantic value of OT hardening words can be immediately transferred to the NT without recognizing different contexts, see Thiselton, *Thiselton on Hermeneutics*, discussing James Barr's criticism of certain articles in *TDNT*: One cannot "lump together the meaning of words drawn from various different contexts, and 'expound' them as the meaning of the word in a given verse," 201. See more discussion in my ch. I, n.5.

6. "Mind," *nous* νοῦς has no equivalent in the OT, although it is often interchangeable with "heart," *kardia*, καρδία, e.g., in the writings of Paul, see Schnelle, *Human Condition*, 105; Bultmann, *Theology 1*, 221; Taylor, "Humanity," 321, 323.

7. See my ch. I, n11 on the "neck" as a metaphor taken from the draft animal, whose efforts to resist are localized in the neck.

The Hardening of Gentiles

The apostle Paul in addressing the Roman church around 57 CE[8] announces the need of God's righteousness for the gentiles in Romans 1. Paul describes those who worship the creation instead of the creator and "suppress (*katechō* κατέχω) the truth" because of their blindness (Rom 1:18, 21–23; cf. Wis 13:1–9). "They became futile in their thinking (ἐματαιώθησαν ἐν τοῖς διαλογισμοῖς αὐτῶν; aorist passive of *mataioō*, ματαιόω, with dative of *dialogismos*, διαλογισμός) and their foolish hearts were darkened (ἐσκοτίσθη ἡ ἀσύνετος αὐτῶν καρδία; passive of *skotizō* σκοτίζω)" (Rom 1:21). The dullness and blindness of their understanding is underscored here. For similar thematic word combinations see LXX Jeremiah 5:21, 23; 16:12 (to Israel and Judah). For example: "a senseless and heartless people" (λαὸς μωρὸς καὶ ἀκάρδιος, Jer 5:21), "an unresponsive and disobedient heart" (καρδία ἀνήκοος καὶ ἀπειθής, v. 23), "of your evil heart not to obey me" (τῆς καρδίας ὑμῶν τῆς πονηρᾶς τοῦ μὴ ὑπακούειν μου, Jer 16:12).

Paul declares that God has punished these gentiles to sin further. God has "handed them over to sin" (Rom 1:24, 26). This pronouncement reflects the similar concept of YHWH's hardening of Israel as seen in post-exilic Third Isaiah (64:6–7). The plight of the hardened gentile in Romans 1 is a judgment of hardening where they can apparently do nothing but sin. God is the cause of hardening that results from or presupposes the gentiles' sinfulness.

In Ephesians (ca. 85 CE), a disciple of Paul recalls to his readers their previously sinful state where they "were darkened in the understanding (ἐσκοτωμένοι τῇ διανοίᾳ perfect passive participle of *skotoō* σκοτόω) due to their hardness of heart (διὰ τὴν πώρωσιν τῆς καρδίας αὐτῶν Eph 4:18). This condition is their sinful state of hardness, God as the cause is implied in the perfect passive participle (*eskotōmenoi* ἐσκοτωμένοι). This teaching on the old life provides a constrast and prepares the way for walking in the new life (4:25—5:21).

---

8. Paul's Letter to the Romans is written from Cenchrea, sea port of Corinth, ca. 57 CE; Rom 15:25; 16:1; Acts 20:2–3, before his final trip to Jerusalem Acts 20:16, see Puskas and Reasoner, *Letters of Paul*, 60.

The Hardening of Israel

The problem of Israel's unbelief surfaces in the ministry of Jesus as well as the missionary activity of the early church. I will first investigate the hardening of Israel in the Gospels.[9] In disputes with the Pharisees regarding the healing activity of Jesus on the Sabbath, Jesus was "angered" and "grieved" at his critics' "hardness (*pōrōsis*, πώρωσις) of heart" (Mark 3:5). There is some duality in Mark's conception of hardness of heart. It is a sin that angers Jesus (3:5; 8:17–18) and an affliction for which he was "grieved" (3:5). Elsewhere, hardness of heart can even affect the sincere or well-intentioned disciples (6:52; 8:17–18).[10]

Was it in response to this dilemma of Israel's unbelief that the church turned to the prophetic statement of Isaiah 6:9-10? This hardening pronouncement is first found in Mark 4:11-12 with regard to Jesus' teaching in parables (written ca. 75 CE).

Mark's paraphrase abbreviates the Isaiah 6 text. Mark has placed the part that derives from Isaiah 6:9 in *the third person*, while the LXX follows the second person. The clauses of Isaiah 6:9 are *reversed* in Mark's quotation, with the "seeing" clause occurring first and the "hearing" clause second. Mark also leaves out the blindness of the eyes, the deafness of the ears, and the undiscerning heart found in Isaiah 6:10.[11] For Mark "the heart

---

9. On literary features, key concerns, dating (post-70 CE), and other questions, see Puskas and Crump, *Gospels and Acts*. A recent work argues that the Gospels were written about a notable Judean figure (Jesus) whose wonderworking and prophetic teachings had particular purchase after the destruction of the temple by literary authors who wrote in competition with one another, see Walsh, *Origins*. Certainly those aspects of artistic creation and literary competition (Luke 1:1-4; John 20:30-31) are present in these post-70 writings, but we also find data that: (a) appear to address felt-needs of community life and worship (Matt 18:15-20; 28:19-20) and (b) assume the reverence for Jesus the Messiah (Mark 14:22-25/1 Cor 11:23-26; Matt 16:16; Luke 24:44-48; John 20:28-31). This data suggests that the authors and their readers were both community members that share a similar faith (not unlike Paul and his intended readers). Perhaps the competition of the Gospel writers reflects that found among different faith communities (e.g., Markan, Lukan), not unlike the competition for recognition or enlistment that we find among confessional/denominational groups today (e.g., Baptists, Lutheran). I do not regard this competition to be as divisive as the "Pauline vs. Petrine communities" devised by F. C. Baur, see Hill, *Hellenists and Hebrews*. See also Davies, and Allison, *Matthew 2*, 781-91; and Hurtado, *Lord Jesus Christ*.

10. Marcus, *Mark 1-8*, 253. Even though the disciples of Jesus are Judeans (of *historic* Israel), they are Christ-following believers and thus members of the nascent church, to be discussed later.

11. Evans, *To See and Not Perceive*, 91-92. Evans notes, on p. 105, that Mark 4:11-12

is one's personal center, where one can decide for faith in the gospel (11:23) or harden one's heart and keep one's distance (8:17)."[12]

Mark 4:11-12 appears to be an independent logion[13] that may even reflect misunderstandings in Mark's own audience. For example: was Jesus' intention in the parables to confuse most listeners so that only a few (Mark's readers?) could understand them (cf. Mark 7:17-18)? The conjunctions *hina* "so that" and the *mēpote* "lest" both convey purpose.[14] Did the confused reception of the parables in Mark confirm this purpose? The Isaianic quote functions for Mark to explain why Jesus speaks in parables. It continues the theme of the unrecognized Messiah among the people (Mark 3:13—6:6a).[15] It underscores the reality of two classes of hearers: the believers and unbelievers. Yet the disciples also appear to fall under the latter class (see warning in Mark 4:24-25). An affective reading of Mark 4:11-12 drives home this opacity to all who read Mark's Gospel

> We are not merely *told* about those who "see and yet do not see," *we are given the opportunity to experience this for ourselves.* The reader lives through the experience of being shut out of insight and understanding by an opaque veil, followed by the gift of a modest amount of sight and understanding, in a surprising

---

has similarities with Tg. Isa. 6:9-10, both are concerned with outsiders who will not listen. In MT Isa 6:9-10 "say to *this* people." Both mention "forgiven" *not* "healed" as in MT Isa. Both 1QIsaᵃ and LXX agree with MT Isa 6 ("this people . . . healed"). Matthew 13:14-15 following Mark 4:11-12 is concerned "with them" (outsiders) but quotes LXX Isa 6:9b-10 and thus retains "heal" (v. 15c).

12. Schnelle, *Theology*, 421.

13. Isa 6:10 along with other LXX texts, e.g., Exod 16:4; Pss 22: 41:9; 77:24 (NRSV: 78:24); 95:7-11; 117:25-26 (NRSV: 118:25-26); Isa 40:3; 49:6; 53; Zech 12:10 may have been part of an early Christian collection of Israel's Scriptures (i.e., testimonia) used to support Jesus as the Messiah and the mission of the early church. See Dodd, *Scriptures*; and Albl, *Testimonia*.

14. Marcus examines other options from Aramaic softening the Greek *hina* clause (cf. Manson, *Teaching of Jesus*, 75-80), but concludes (with Black, *Aramaic Approach*, 212-14) that the Aramaic *dĕ* followed by *dilĕmma* suggests purpose, in his *Mark 1-8*, 299-300.

15. I follow here a dramatic plot structure of Complication: Who is Jesus? (Mark 1:1—8:26), Crisis: Jesus the Messiah (8:27—10:52), and Denouement: the Messiah must suffer and die (11:1—16:8), in Puskas and Crump, *Gospels and Acts*, 84-85. The accounts of restoring sight (8:22-26; 10:46-52), to be discussed later, are significant transitional stories in my outline.

reversal of position with those who had started out on the favored side of the veil.¹⁶

If Mark 4:11-12 addresses Israel's unbelief, it also draws in its readers to identify and empathize with this plight of unbelief into which even followers of Jesus may easily fall (cf. Heb 3:12-13).

In the debate of Jesus with the Pharisees over divorce, both Matthew 19:8 and Mark 10:5 refer to Moses allowing divorce because of the hardness of the Israelites' hearts (*sklērokardia*). Although directed at his Jewish critics, it may also address the shortcomings of the Mosaic law to adequately address the failings of marriage in ancient Israel.¹⁷

> He fiercely protested against the use of Torah and *hălākâ* to protect hardness of heart: the taken-for-granted practice of divorce (Mark 10:1–12 = Matt 19:1–12) and the spuriously pious refusal to help one's parents in need (Mark 7:10-12 = Matt 15:3-6).¹⁸

The mysteries of the kingdom that are made known to the disciples and hidden from outsiders¹⁹ may signify that the kingdom of God has emerged in the ministry of Jesus. This is why Mark places this logion (Mark 4:11-12) in the context of the kingdom parables. When this mystery of God's kingdom in Jesus is not understood or perceived, God hardens them. This observation explains the presence of this logion among the kingdom parables and why Mark has placed it into a missionary context (3:13—6:7), which begins with the choosing of "missionaries" and ends with the sending out of missionaries.

---

16. Fowler, "Rhetoric of Direction," 131. In Ap. Jas. 7.1-7 (NHC I,2), Jesus expresses frustration with his disciples, who do not perceive even when he speaks to them openly (not in parables).

17. "No judgment pronounced in the light of the Law can be merciful. Such judgments give him no real help, whether severe or lenient. On the contrary, such judgments usually harden him, leaving him indifferent or defiant as he was before. Since the New Testament judgment on man derives from the mercy and help already given to him, it is itself *eo ipso* merciful and helpful. It measures man by what God has done for him, by what Jesus Christ has accomplished in his place for his justification and deliverance from this burden, for his peace and salvation." Karl Barth, *Church Dogmatics III/2*, 605.

18. Meyer, "Jesus," 791.

19. On "outsiders" in Qumran (1QH 5.36); heretics in rabbinica (m. Meg 4.8), non-Pythagoreans (Iamblichus, *Life of Pythagoras* 35.242), and unbelievers in early Christianity (1 Cor 5:12-13; 1 Thess 4:12; Col 4:5; cf. 1 Tim 3:7; Rev 22:14-15; 2 Clem 13:1) as cited in Marcus, *Mark 1-8*, 298-99. Although the boundaries fluctuate, see also "in-group and out-group" in Malina and Rohrbaugh, *Social-Science*, 373-74.

Later in the context of missionary activity hardening was an explanation of Israel's unbelief in the face of the gospel message. In Mark's Gospel we see that hardening is not only a fact but a divine intention all along (cf. *hina* of purpose with *mēpote* in Mark 4:12). Is the hardening permanent or temporary? Mark does not appear to address this issue.

In Luke 8:10, the writer (ca. 80 CE) uses the Isaiah 6 quote but shows that it was Jesus' intention to manifest light (8:16–18) and to open the eyes of the blind (4:18 [Isa 42:7]; Luke 7:22[Isa 35:5]). Luke's quotation of Isaiah 6:9–10 is more succinct and seeks to clarify its meaning, making it less enigmatic than Mark 4:11–12. Luke maintains the divine intention in Luke 8:10, but may have condensed the quotation to anticipate the day of Pentecost (Acts 2:14–42) when Israel would hear the gospel and be given more opportunity to respond to the gospel. After repeated Jewish rejection to the gospel proclaimed by Paul and his associates (Acts 13:44–46; 18:6), a hardening judgment is pronounced on unbelieving Israel (Acts 28:23–28) to legitimize (I think) the Christian mission to the gentiles.[20]

This indictment on Jewish unbelief in Acts 28 is comparable to the closing invective upon the Judeans in Stephen's speech (7:51–53). In both accounts the unbelief is portrayed as a hardening of the ears and heart (7:51; Exod 33:5; Acts 28:26–27; Isa 6:9–10). In both the current unbelief of the Jews is interpreted as the disobedience typical of Israel's history ("your fathers"; 7:51b–52; 28:25b). In both there is a sweeping pronouncement on impenitent Israel for its current and historic unbelief.[21]

The people of Israel (Judeans associated with torah, temple, and synagogue) were given numerous opportunities to respond to the gospel and now the early church turns to the gentiles. This quote at the end of Acts shows this movement to the "nations" in the church was part of God's plan in salvation history (cf. LXX Isa 42:6; 49:6; 52:10; 60:3; Luke 2:32; 4:25–28; 24:47; Acts 13:47; 28:28). Luke, focused on the present mission, does not appear to have a hope for *all* Israel to be saved, as Paul had

---

20. "Isaiah's words were directed against those who steadfastly 'refused to believe'" in Puskas, *Conclusion*, 23n60 citing Cassidy, *Politics*, 130. It is noteworthy from Acts 28:24 and, e.g., 13:43; 14:1; 15:5; 17:1,4, 12; 18:8; 23:6, that some Judeans *believed* the gospel. On the nature and extent of Luke's redactional activity here, see Llewelyn and Kearnsley, *New Documents 7*, 91–92.

21. O'Toole, "Why Write Acts?" 67. The second indicting address of Stephen "you ... uncircumcised in hearts and ears" *aperitmētos kardia kai tois ōsin* ἀπερίτμητος καρδίᾳ καὶ τοῖς ὠσίν, Acts 7:51, draws upon similar metaphorical language in the Greek OT, e.g., Lev 26:41; Deut 10:16; 30:6; Jer 4:4; 6:10; 9:25 LXX. Beale and Carson, *Commentary*, 569.

expressed it (Rom 11:26–27). The concluding statement in Acts 28:30 "he welcomed all (*pantas* πάντας) who came to him" at Rome, however, appears to include individual Jews as well as gentiles who would constitute the remnant of righteous Israel.[22]

"Israel's destiny can be fulfilled only in a new creation beyond this age ... a *preparation* for the End: when God's people is wholly taken into God and Israel's hopes are thereby fulfilled."[23]

Matthew 13:10–13 uses the LXX Isaiah 6:9–10 quote[24] to show that those who oppose the words and deeds of Jesus are outside the kingdom of heaven (ca. 85 CE). Matthew uses the antithetic parallelism "to you" and "to them" (v. 11) that makes the distinction between: (a) the disciples who know God's mystery of the kingdom in Jesus (something the prophets longed to see, 13:16–17), and (b) those (Pharisaic Jews?) who refuse to believe and have been hardened (from them the blessings of God's kingdom will be taken away, 13:12–13; cf. Matt 3:8–9//Luke 3:8).[25] Matthew highlights this distinction by including here the logia in v. 12 "from him who has not, even what he has will be taken away." Luke following Mark has this saying *later* in the discourse (Luke 8:18; Mark 4:25). Next, the language of Isaiah 6:9 is summarized in Matthew 13:13 and then the passage is formally quoted in vv. 14–15. The LXX quote could be a later interpolation to further underscore the fact that Israel's hardening (and gentile reception) is in fulfillment of prophecy and was therefore God's intention, all along.[26] The tension of Jesus with the Jewish leadership of his

---

22. Puskas, *Conclusion*, 78n39. See also Acts 15:5; 18:8; 23:6; 28:24a. On remnant, see my ch. I, n105, if there is to be a righteous remnant, it is a result of God's grace (cf. Rom 11:5). Kinzer finds hope in Luke-Acts for Jerusalem and the Jewish people because of the crucified and risen Messiah, *Jerusalem Crucified, Jerusalem Risen*, 3–4.

23. Reflecting upon Luke 1:69–70 and Rom 11:13–24, Jenson, *Systematic Theology* 2, 170–71. See also Kaminsky and Reasoner, "Israel's Election," 421–44. "Paul affirms Jesus as Messiah while affirming that the physical descendants of Israel remain God's people who still are heir of God's covenants." Ibid., 446.

24. LXX Isa 6:10, used by Matthew, has 3rd pl. aor. indic. (*kammyō* καμμύω) and subj. verbs in Isa 6:10 (e.g., ἴδωσιν *idōsin*), but no IMV verbs (e.g., *shāmēn* שָׁמֵן) that are used as we have in the MT. These changes lessen the force of the Heb. text. See my ch. I, n56.

25. Alluding to this text, a distinction between insiders and outsiders is a key theme in the NHL: 2 Apoc Jas 51:14–19; 60:5–12 (NHC V 4); Apoc Pet 73:11–17 (NHC VII 3); Test Truth 48:8–15 (NHC IX 3). Recalling the division of the faithful and stubbornly disobedient in the DSS, a division that will remain until the last days: e.g., 1QS IV, 2–18. See also my ch. II, n18.

26. Luz, *Matthew 8–20*, 246–47.

day may also reflect a later situation between the communities of Matthew in conflict with certain Judean groups (ca. 80 CE).[27]

Let us now examine the writings of Paul on the hardening of Israel (mid-first century CE). In contrast to his ministry of the new covenant (2 Cor 3:3; alluding to LXX Ezek 11:19; 36:26), Paul, in 2 Corinthians 3:14-16, writes that the minds (*noēma* νόημα) of unbelieving Israel were hardened (*pōroō*)[28] and that they read the old covenant (cf. Exod 24:7) with a veil (*kalymma* κάλυμμα) that shielded Israel from God's glory (2 Cor 3:13), a veil that only Christ can set aside (ca. 56 CE).

On this pericope, David E. Garland comments

> A chorus of biblical witnesses ascribes the inability to see and hear to a sinful condition (see Isa 6:9-10; 29:10-12; Jer 5:21-24; Ezek 12:2; Mark 4:10-12; John 12:39-40; Acts 28:25-27). Paul uses the noun form of the verb "to harden" in Rom 11:25 to explain why most of Israel has failed to respond to the gospel: "A hardening has come upon Israel" (see Rom 11:7-8). In the context of his argument here, Paul implies that any who fail to see God's glory manifest in his own ministry of the Spirit are in the same hardened condition as Israel of old.[29]

Paul in 2 Corinthians 4:3-4 resumes the veil theme (3:14-16) and states: "the god of this world has blinded [*typhloūn*, τυφλοῦν] the minds of the unbelieving Israel, to keep them from seeing the light of the gospel." Thus, we have here in 3:14 and 4:4 the two verbs of " blinded" and

---

27. The Greek *Ioudaios*, often rendered "Jews," is best translated "Judeans," an ethnic group connected to the land of Judea (Gk., *Ioudaia*), Jerusalem, and its temple (BDAG, 478). It also applies to Judeans of Galilee or those Graeco-Judeans of the diaspora ("dispersed" outside of Judea, Josephus, *Apion* 2.38-39). Christ-followers of the first two centuries were either Judean or gentile followers of Jesus the Messiah. Both groups considered themselves as members of the Israelite faith (an insider self-designation). Both Philo (*Prob.* 175-91) and Josephus (*War* 2.119, 166; *Ant.* 18.11-12) describe certain subsets of the Judeans (e.g., Essenes, Pharisees) as philosophical groups. See Elliott, "Jesus the Israelite," and Mason, "Jews, Judaeans." There is still considerable debate on this matter, so at times I will use "Jews/Judeans" to refer to the Jews of the Second Temple period. For more discussion, see my Appx., n28.

28. The verb *pōroō* is also in Rom 11:7 to indicate that the chosen received grace and the rest (unfaithful Israel) were hardened, and also in John 12:40 where the Isa 6:10 is employed as Jesus approaches his final days in Jerusalem (cf. John 1:10-12). Paul's use of *kardia*, often synonymous with *nous* ("mind" which has no OT equivalent) stands in the tradition of OT anthropology, see Wolff, *Anthropology*, 40-58, cited in Schnelle, *Theology*, 316 n358. See also my ch. II, n6.

29. Garland, *2 Corinthians*, 191, see also his discussion in 189-92.

"hardened" (*typhloūn/pōroun*, τυφλοῦν/πωροῦν), both of which are found in John 12:40.[30] In 2 Corinthians 3:14-16, a divine agency as the cause is implied with the aorist passive of πωρόω *pōroō* ("was hardened," v. 14), but in 2 Corinthians 4:3-4, the "god of this world" (cf. 1 Cor 2:6, 8; Eph 2:2) has blinded the minds of unbelievers (Jews *and* gentiles). The actions of God are not merely displaced or transferred to another power. Paul, agreeing with, for example, Philo (*Conf.* 171-82), Rule of the Community (1QS III, 15-21), Sirach 33:11-13, and the Testament of Judah 19:4, assumes that one sovereign God, has commissioned many lesser powers and ministering angels to serve his purposes.[31]

Following Ernst Käsemann, Romans 9-11 can be outlined as: introduction (9:1-5); the validity and provisional goal of divine election (9:6-29); Israel's unbelief (9:30—10:21); and the mystery of salvation history (11:1-36). The three major divisions of Romans 9-11 reflect the past, present, and future, i.e., Israel's past election, present unbelief, and future restoration. The obduracy idea runs throughout these chapters of Romans (ca. 57 CE).[32]

In Romans 9-11 Paul responds to the questions: Has God rejected his people, Israel? And has Paul forgotten Israel in his work among the gentiles? Paul underscores the fact that God alone determines salvation (Rom 9:17-18; cf. Exod 9:16) and so a remnant of Israel, alongside believing gentiles, will emerge (9:27-29; 11:5) in support of a divine mission.[33]

Citing the Greek (LXX) Isaiah 29:10 (*pneuma katanyxeōs* πνεῦμα κατανύξεως), Deuteronomy 29:3 (cf. Isa 6:9-10), and Psalm 68:23-24 (NRSV 69:23-24), Paul argues that "a hardening God has come upon part

---

30. Evans, *To See and Not Perceive*, 83-84. See also 11Q11 V.6-7, To a demon: "Your face is a face of [delus]ion, and your horns (קרן *qeren*) are horns of illu[si]on (חֲלוֹם *ḥălôm* חֲלוֹם). You are darkness (*ḥōshak* חושך) and not light."

31. Citations from Furnish, *II Corinthians*, 220-21; and Stuckenbruck, *Rebellious Angels*, 232-35, 270.

32. Käsemann, *Romans*, 253-321. "The proper reading and interpretation of Romans is ... of acknowledging the choice and election of this people, of recognizing the 'firstness' of this enigmatic and empirically undefinable community as sign of the Godhead of God." In Harrisville, *Romans*, 29. On "mystery" (e.g., Rom 11:25) as a divine matter "too profound for human ingenuity," see BDAG 661-62. See also Evans, *To See and Not Perceive*, 84.

33. "To the question, 'Has God rejected his people?' Paul gives a negative answer (11:1). Paul then goes on to show that the rejection of Israel by God is partial (11:1-10), temporary (11:11-27), and has had a deeper purpose (11:28-36)," Myers, "Romans," 824. See also my Appx., n5.

of Israel until the full number of the gentiles has arrived" (Rom 11:25). Nevertheless: "Instead of being consigned to eternal ignorance, Israel is now portrayed as 'stunned,' a condition from which they may be already starting to recover."[34]

Paul believes that his work will bring about the salvation of Israel by making the Jews jealous. (1) Jewish unbelief, leads to (2) salvation of gentiles, leads to (3) salvation of all Israel. The hardening is God's intention but it is only *temporary* to prepare for the fullness of the gentiles, then all Israel will be saved (Rom 11:25-29; cf. 15:9-13).[35] "Paul affirms Jesus as Messiah while affirming that the physical descendants of Israel remain God's people who still are heir of God's covenants."[36]

In John 12:40, an editorial comment at the conclusion of the Book of Signs, the Fourth Evangelist (ca. 90 CE) makes an evaluation of the ministry of Jesus and notes that "the Judeans" (Jewish opponents of Jesus) could not believe the signs, and even the sign of life in the raising Lazarus and prompted their efforts to have Jesus killed. The free quotation of Isaiah 6:9-10 in John adds reference to "blinded eyes" and "hardened hearts" further capturing the hardening imagery of the passage. The Fourth Gospel has cited this hardening pronouncement with divine causation to explain why many "could not believe" (12:39; cf. 1:11). John 12:40 omits "hearing" to focus more on seeing/sight a key theme in his gospel (1:14, 18, 34, 38-39, 46; 9:39; 11:35; 14:9; 20:25).[37]

Earlier, in John 9, Jesus the "light of the world" (v. 5) heals a man born blind from birth, but his healing from blindness and his growing

---

34. Jewett et al., *Romans*, 663n126, citing Stanley, *Scripture*, 161.

35. In Rom 11:25-26a, Nanos, citing ancient medical texts (e.g., Hippocrates, *De Fractures* 23.10; *De Articulus* 15.6; Galen, *Ars Medica* 1.387; Celsus, *De Medicina*), argues that "a protective callus has formed on Israel" until the full number of the gentiles comes in "then all Israel will be healed" in his *Reading Romans 2*, 153-78. Dunn also includes as an optional rendering of *pōrōsis* "a callus which unites a fractured bone," *Romans 9-16*, 640. See also my ch. II, n4.

36. Kaminsky and Reasoner, "Israel's Election," 446. Written in response to N. T. Wright's redefinition of "all Israel" as comprised only of Messiah-believing gentiles and Jews. See Wright, *Paul and Faithfulness*, 1244-45. See also my ch. II, n23.

37. Thompson, *John*, 275. She also cites here the importance of sight (firsthand experience) over hearing (secondhand experience) according to Greek philosophers (Heraclitus) and certain historians (e.g., Polybius, Herodotus, Thucydides, Josephus). The Evangelist has Jesus pronounce a blessing on those who have not seen, yet believe (20:29), perhaps referring to readers of his gospel (ca. 90 CE). On "seeing" and "not seeing," "knowing" and "not knowing" in ancient drama, see also Seale, *Vision and Stagecraft*.

recognition of Jesus provides a noteworthy contrast to his Judean critics who become spiritually blind to this sign of healing that reveals the identity of Jesus, as the One sent from the Father.

> Jesus, because he is the Sent One . . . gives light to a man who has never seen. But the physical miracle is only the beginning of a longer journey of faith that leads from his understanding of Jesus as "the man called Jesus" (v. 11) to his falling before the Son of Man whom he sees and hears, confessing, "Lord, I believe" (v. 38). "The Jews" who turned toward the Holy of Holies each day to celebrate their unswerving loyalty to the one true God, but who have rejected Jesus' claims to be the revelation of the Father, are now condemned because of their gradual movement into blindness and darkness. Jesus condemns them as blind (vv. 39–41).[38]

After healing the man born blind, Jesus announces with an eye on his Judean critics: "I came into this world for judgment so that those who do not see may see, and does who do see may become blind" (9:39). Rudolf Bultmann finds here a parallel from later Mandaean literature: "I put it before his eyes, but he would not see, I showed him, but he would not see with his eyes."[39]

For the Evangelist, God has hardened the Jews/Judeans so that they could not believe in Jesus as Messiah. This hardening statement regarding the Judean critics of Jesus may reflect some tension between church and synagogue when the Fourth Gospel was written (late first century CE).[40] Some did not openly confess Jesus as Messiah lest they be put out of the synagogue (John 9:22; 12:42; 16:2). Jesus the Word is light and life for the entire world (1:1–4; 3:16–17; 4:42; 6:14; 8:12; 12:47). "Jesus provoked Jews and Gentiles to an ultimate rejection of God that *God* turned into the ultimate means whereby his relationship with his people could be affirmed, healed and restored."[41]

---

38. Moloney, *Signs and Shadows*, 140. "I came into this world, in order that (*hina*) those who do not see should see, and those who see should be blind," John 9:39.

39. Mandaean *Book of John* 175, 24–25 (eighth century CE) in Bultmann, *John*, 340n4.

40. The following work argued for the separation of church and synagogue when the Fourth Gospel was written: Martyn, *History and Theology*, 56–66. The following works acknowledge tension, but not eventful separation: Kimelman, "Birkat ha-Minim," 226–44; and Katz, "Separation," 43–76; Charlesworth, *John*, 43–45. For more discussion, see Puskas and Robbins, *Conceptual Worlds*, 27n46, 76, 84n5.

41. Goldingay, *Letting OT Speak*, 177. Italics in this paradoxical statement are mine.

Miroslav Volf makes a distinction between differentiation and exclusion. Differentiation establishes discreet identity through a process of separating and binding together (cf. Gen 1:3–5, 27). It is the interaction of the self with the other. Exclusion cuts the bonds that connect. Exclusion perceives the other as an enemy or a nonentity. The gospel embraces the other, even if it is perceived as different or no longer innocent (Matt 5:44; Rom 3:23–24).[42]

The hardening of believers

Mark not only applies hardness of heart to "those outside," but *also* to the disciples (perfect passive of *pōroō* πωρόω in 6:52; 8:17).[43]

> Jesus' accusation of the disciples in 8:18a leads into this miracle story. The reader has followed the increasing blindness of the disciples. They have moved from their initial unconditional response to Jesus' call (see 1:16–20; 3:13–19) into lack of understanding (4:10, 13, 23; 5:16, 31; 6:7–30, 37; 8:4), unbelief (4:40–41), hardness of heart (6:52), and a dangerous proximity to the leaven of the Pharisees and the Herodians (8:11–21). Jesus' accusations in 8:17–21 are well-grounded! But in 8:21 he asks whether they did "not yet" understand. There is hope that they may still move from the blindness of their unfaith into true sight. The miracle story of 8:22–26 is a paradigm of that possibility, and plays an important literary function in setting the agenda for the rest of the Gospel.[44]

The two-stage healing of the blind man of Bethsaida (8:22–26) looks backward and forward.[45] It looks *backward* at the hardened hearts of the disciples who "fail to see" and "fail to hear" (8:17–18), despite: the feeding of the five thousand (6:30–44) and the healing of the deaf mute (7:32–35),

---

42. Volf, *Exclusion and Embrace*, on distinctions, 64–67, on gospel, 85.

43. See chart on Insiders and Outsiders in Mark's Gospel in Marcus, *Mark 1–8*, 303–4. See also Fowler, "Rhetoric of Direction," 131, who regards Mark 4:11–12 as also "drawing" Mark's implied readers, perhaps as a warning, that they too could experience spiritual blindness (cf. Heb 3:7–8). See also my ch. II, n16.

44. Moloney, *Mark*, 164. Even in the post-Markan longer ending (ca. 180 CE or later) the risen Jesus upbraids the disciples for their unbelief and "hardness of heart," (*sklērokardia* σκληροκαρδία), Mark 16:14, Ibid., 356–62.

45. The "Janus-like quality" of Mark 8:22–26, is derived from Meier, *Marginal Jew 2*, 691–93. On the symbolic significance of physical disability as it relates to social issues, see my ch. I, n102.

along with the feeding of the four thousand (8:1–10). Mark 8:22–26, which has a two-stage healing, also looks *forward* to the gradual healing of the spiritual vision of Jesus' disciples: the confession of Peter at Caesarea Philippi that Jesus is the Messiah (8:27–30) and the passion predictions (8:31–33; 9:31–32; 10:33–34, 43) ending in the healing of blind Bartimaeus (10:46–52) whose "faith" has made him well (v. 52).

The mystery of Jesus' messiahship resides in his passion and death (Mark 8:34–38; 9:9–13; 15:36–39; 16:6–7), and when this truth is not perceived by the disciples, they too are hardened. Here, not on grounds of disobedience, but because of their spiritual blindness and dullness.[46] Only the Markan context of a suffering Messiah provides the true perspective on the purpose and mission of Jesus.

The New Testament writings are replete with warnings to the believer to remain faithful.[47] Paul admonishes his churches in Galatia and Corinth not to be led astray from the gospel that he has proclaimed to them (e.g., Gal 1:6; 3:1–5; 1 Cor 1:10–11; 2 Cor 13:5; ca. 53–55 CE). John of Patmos (ca. 95 CE) warns those churches in Ephesus and Laodicea that they have "lost their first love" and have "cooled down" in their faithfulness (Rev 2:4; 3:15). In the late first century, the authors of 2 Peter (2:1–22) and 1 John (1:10; 2:4; 4:20) express anguish and consternation for those in their midst who misbehave or who are being misled. The author of 1 John even regards those who have left his community as opponents (2:19, 26).[48] Based on literary and historical precedent, believers who do not heed the admonishments, would meet the conditions for a pronouncement of divine hardening by the NT authors. From the examples that I've provided in this paragraph, I can only speculate about how extensive was the noncompliance.

Hebrews (ca. 90 CE) is an anonymous, early Christian sermon (e.g., 3:1—4:13; 8:1—10:18; 12:1–13; cf. 1 Pet, 2 Clem., Ep. to Diogn. 11–12).[49] In

---

46. Recalling an incident that I overheard: Nurse Kris was seated at the recovery station where I was wheeled right after prostate surgery. Kris was staring at a computer screen while speaking on the phone and saying: "I'm looking, but I can't see it!" (She couldn't find the tab for departmental reports on the hospital website!). It was a communication problem. Although, in Mark's instance the spiritual dullness is similar to what Paul writes about in 1 Cor 2:14, i.e., a lack of spiritual discernment.

47. See admonishments and warnings in many NT instances of "paraenesis." Soulen, *Biblical Criticism*, 149–50; Puskas and Reasoner, *Letters of Paul*, 134–35.

48. Puskas, *Hebrews*, 122–23.

49. See Puskas, *Hebrews*, 122–23, on the genre of Hebrews, 11–14, and on anonymous authorship, 31–33.

this homily, the possibility of Christians, members of God's house (3:5–6), to harden their hearts is evident (3:8, 15; 4:7).

Craig Koester observes

> Hardness of heart is a metaphor for those who refuse to do God's will (Deut 10:16; 2 Kgs 17:14; Rom 2:5; cf. Zech 7:12; Jer 17:23). The metaphor often warned people not to repeat the sins of their ancestors (Neh 9:16–17, 29; 2 Chron 30:8; Jer 7:26; Acts 19:9). If Pharaoh hardened his heart before the exodus (Exod 8:15, 32; 9:34), Moses' generation did so afterward.[50]

In quoting Ps. 95:7–11 (Ps 94:7b-11 LXX) "harden not your hearts,"[51] Hebrews 3:7—4:7 shows that since Moses could not prevent his people from losing their inheritance, the writer of Hebrews warns his readers not to fall into the *same* dilemma and lose their heavenly inheritance (the first generation that did not enter the promised land). Here, as in the Psalms, Israel's rebelliousness serves as a moral lesson for the listener/reader to avoid such behavior.

> The text cited is the final portion of Ps 95, a hymn that praises the sovereign power of Yahweh and invites the worshiper to adore God and to hear God's voice. The appeal is followed by the challenge of these verses to the Israelite community not to be like the desert generation, who had hardened their hearts and not attained the promised land of rest.[52]

New Testament Summation

The New Testament writers were more selective in their use of the Old Testament language of hardening (see my ch. I, Lexical Terms), having their own agenda and purposes. Nevertheless, as in the Old Testament, the hardness of heart motif reflects an inability and refusal to understand.

Paul takes up the hardening pronouncement on the gentiles who tend to worship the creature rather than the Creator (Rom 1:18, 21–23; cf. Wis 13). His language of "handing over" the gentiles is reminiscent of the language in Third Isaiah regarding Israel (64:6–7). Later, in Ephesians

---

50. Koester, *Hebrews*, 255. See, e.g., Deut 31:27.

51. Negative with present, subjunctive μὴ σκληρύνητε *mē sklērynēte* citing LXX Ps 94.

52. Attridge, *Hebrews*, 115. Ps 95 is Ps 94 in the Greek OT (LXX).

4:18, readers are warned not to return (v. 17) to their bleak and destitute former lives.

In contrast to the ministry of the new covenant (2 Cor 3:3; LXX Ezek 11:19; 36:26), Paul in 2 Corinthians 3:14–16 and 4:3–4 uses hardening language to describe Israel's blindness to the gospel (55 CE). Second Corinthians 4:3–4 appears to include both Jewish and gentile unbelievers.

In Romans 9–11, Paul addressed the unbelief of Israel in relation to God's salvation history (57 CE). The hardening of Israel is temporary to prepare for the fullness of the gentiles, then all Israel will be saved (11:25–29; 15:9–13). Citing the Greek (LXX) Deuteronomy 29:3, Isaiah 29:10 (*katanyxis* κατάνυξις), and Psalm 68:23–24 (NRSV 69:23–24), Paul argues that God has allowed historic Israel to become hardened to God's revelation for the sake of his gentile mission. Nevertheless: "Instead of being consigned to eternal ignorance, Israel is now portrayed as 'stunned,' a condition from which they may be already starting to recover."[53]

What I stated earlier about the "performative function" of hardening pronouncements on the Judeans (Isa 6:9–10; Acts 28:26–28), also applies to God's promise of salvation to historic Israel (Rom 11:26–27).[54]

"The prophet's word (= the word of Yahweh), like Paul's Word of the cross, is two-edged. It destroys the illusions of self-determination by declaring human wisdom and understanding to be blindness and incomprehension, but it also declares the will of Yahweh to open eyes and unstop ears."[55]

In the Gospels (late-first century CE) the problem of Israel's unbelief is recounted in the ministry of Jesus and seems to reflect some tension between certain Judeans and the early church. Isaiah 6:9–10 is cited in Mark 4:11–12 (composed ca. 75 CE), with parallels in the other Gospels. Isaiah 6 in Luke 8:10 is more succinct, to prepare for a more complete pronouncement in Acts 28 after several attempts at reaching those in the synagogues (13:44–46; 18:6; ca. 80 CE). Written in the late first century, John 12:40 focuses on the blindness of the Judeans who do not recognize the signs performed by the Son (9:39).

---

53. Jewett and Kotansky, *Romans*, 663n126, citing Stanley, *Scripture*, 161. See also II, n34.

54. See speech-act theory and the performative function of certain utterances in *Thiselton on Hermeneutics*, 61–66, 84–86. See also my ch. I, n50.

55. Alexandra Brown discusses the hardening pronouncement of Isa 6:9–11 and its partial repeal in 29:18–21 in the context of Paul's preaching of the cross in 1 Cor 1–2, following the speech-act theory of J. L. Austin, in her *Cross and Human Transformation*, 82.

The hardening of the believers is not ignored. Mark 4:11–12 (implied) and 6:52; 8;17, may reflect concerns about the several misconceptions concerning the messiahship of Jesus. The "Janus-like quality" of the gradual healing of the blind man in Mark 8:22–26 looks backward at the hardened hearts of the disciples (8:17–18) and forward to the eventual spiritual healing of the disciples (8:27–33; 10:52). It makes a narrative connection between the disability of physical blindness and spiritual blindness.

The New Testament is replete with urgent admonitions to remain faithful to the gospel (Gal 1:6; 3:4–5; 1 Cor 1:10–11; Rev 2:4; 3:15). Hebrews 3:8—4:7 is more explicit (ca. 90 CE): harden not your hearts as your spiritual ancestors had done in the wilderness (citing Ps 95 [LXX Ps 94]).

Conclusion

THE HARDNESS OF HEART concerns a self-focused set of responses that is (a) incapable of decisive, self-sacrificial action, (b) reflecting a complete unwillingness to learn and to accept new information.[1] If we just focus on the human aspect here, does hardening reflect resistance based on a biased pre-understanding? "Contempt prior to examination has been called an intellectual vice, from which the greatest faculties of mind are not free."[2] Perhaps it reflects a determined unwillingness to comply because one is "constitutionally incapable of being honest" with oneself?

> Rarely have we seen a person fail who has thoroughly followed our path. *Those who do not recover are people who cannot or will not completely give themselves to this simple program, usually men and women who are constitutionally incapable of being honest with themselves. There are such unfortunates. They are not at fault; they seem to have been born that way. They are naturally incapable of grasping and developing a manner of living which demands rigorous honesty. Their chances are less than average.* There are those, too,

---

1. The verb *pōroō* πωρόω "to cause someone to be completely unwilling to learn and to accept new information," Louw and Nida, *Lexicon*, 332. See my ch. II, n4. On Isaiah 6:10 (MT), see Oswalt, *Isaiah, Chapters 1–39*, 189n10. See my ch. I, n.59.

2. Paley (1743–1805), *Evidences of Christianity*, 102. The quote is one of Paley's observations in response to a demeaning statement in *Roman Annals* by Tacitus the Roman historian (ca. 117) that Christianity is a "pernicious superstition," 15.44.

CONCLUSION

who suffer from grave emotional and mental disorders, but many of them do recover if they have the capacity to be honest.[3]

The hardening terminology in biblical literature has been used to explain different problems and dilemmas faced by Israel and the church. Non-Israelites (gentiles) were hardened so that God could carry out *Heilsgeschichte* and to demonstrate God's righteous and holy standards. When a people became so fixed in unbelief that they would no longer hear God's messengers, they were hardened to show that their disobedience was part of God's plan all along. Above all, God was in control. The God of Israel had a purpose for all the strange phenomena that went on in the world of the ancients. This view of God was the working assumption of the biblical writers.

> It has been concluded that the original Hebrew text of Isa. 6:9-10 was intended to convey the idea that it was God's purpose that his prophet deepen Israel's obduracy. This idea is based upon the conclusion that the verbs of v. 10 were originally hiphil imperatives, as the MT points them. The prophet's word was a harsh word of judgment intended to promote obduracy and to make the people ripe for judgment. This severe word, however, is tempered by the hope of a remnant and restoration, especially as seen in Second and Third Isaiah. The final clause of 6:13, which introduces the positive idea of the remnant as a "holy seed," is likely an effort to relate Isaiah's commission of judgment more closely to Isaiah's remnant idea. (Nevertheless, Isa. 6:9-13b still stands as an unqualified word of obduracy and judgment.)[4]

The textual transmission of Isaiah 6:9-10 shows a marked tendency to move away from the harsh, telic understanding of the Hebrew text. In the LXX and the Targums there appears to be a consistent avoidance to let stand unmodified the idea that YHWH would harden his own people.

---

3. *Alcoholics Anonymous*, 58. Failure to comply with the program is interpreted as an incapacity to be honest with oneself and to avail oneself of what benefits that the program can provide. *Italics* are mine. A similar quote as that from Paley (above) is provided on p. 568, but it is attributed to another later author (Herbert Spencer, philosopher, 1820-1903), possibly a misquotation. In both quotations above, certain truth claims are assumed by the authors.

4. Evans, *To See and Not Perceive*, 163. Although it is retained in 1QIsa^a, the phrase "holy seed" is *not* found in LXX, but a remnant idea is still conveyed "those who have been left . . . a tenth" ([NETS], 830). See my ch. I, n67.

Many of the textual variations were obviously self-serving in their attempts to domesticate God's attitude and activity.[5]

Jesus and several NT writers cite Isaiah 6:9–10 (e.g., Mark 4:12; Luke 8:10; Acts 28:26; Rom 11:8) to explain the mystery of the rejection of Jesus and the apostolic witness to him.[6]

The gospel has been rejected, not simply because its hearers were dull, but because it was and continues to be God's (mysterious) will. The Jewish rejection of Jesus raised for the early Christians the same sort of question raised in the minds of exiled Israel by the prophets. In the case of Israel, there was the conviction that the exile was a purge from which a righteous remnant would emerge. In the case of the church, there was the conviction that Jewish rejection and ostracism unwittingly furthered *God's* purposes in producing a new remnant of the righteous among the gentiles.[7]

A persistent theme is found in biblical literature: "The Lord is not slack concerning his promise, as some men count slackness; but is longsuffering to us-ward, *not* willing that *any* should perish, but that *all* should come to repentance" (2 Pet 3:9; cf. Isa 25:6–8; John 3:16–17; 12:32; 1 Cor 15:28; 2 Cor 5:19; Eph 1:10; 1 Tim 2:4; 4:19; Titus 2:11). In contrast to hardness of heart is the purity of heart (Matt 5:8; cf. Ps 24:4 [Ps 23:4 LXX]), a heart that is innocent and morally "clean" (Ps 51:10; Job 4:7; Hab 1:13). It entails all aspects of receptivity: hearing/heeding, seeing (with the eyes of faith), trusting, and obeying, Again is it God's doing or that of the individual, or both?[8]

As the apostle Paul tells us "For we see in a mirror dimly" or "indirectly" (δι' ἐσόπτρου ἐν αἰνίγματι, *di esoptrou en ainigmati*; Lat., *per speculum in enigmate*, 1 Cor 13:12).[9] Our historical and literary knowledge is partial. We live in a modern industrial age of computer technology with air travel, great advances in medicine, and space exploration. On the other hand, there is the biblical world: it was fundamentally an agrarian culture of wheel and plow with travel by sail or domesticated animal, with much disease and a high mortality rate. Our understanding of the historical and literary perspectives is limited. For example, are we discussing the perspective of the prophet

---

5. Evans, *To See and Not Perceive*, 163–64.

6. See my ch. II, n13 on an early Christian collection of Israel's Scriptures (i.e., testimonia) used to support Jesus as the Messiah and the mission of the early church.

7. Evans, *To See and Not Perceive*, 164–65. On remnant, see my ch. I, n105.

8. On faith as trust and receptivity to the divine message, see: Brueggemann, *Faith*, 76–79; Hays, "Faith," 1129–33; Gupta, "Faith."

9. Kittel, "Αἴνιγμα (ἔσοπτρον)," 178–180.

regarding his audience, the perspective of the final author concerning the prophet and his audience, the perspectives of the audience of the prophet, the perspectives of the audience who heard the book read, the perspectives of the readers who read the book? On what level is communication adequately received between the addresser and addressee?

Who is hardened? Why are they hardened? Do "the hardened" conceive of themselves as hardened? Did the readers/audience of the prophetic book identify with the perspective of the prophet (e.g., Isaiah of Jerusalem) regarding who is hardened? Was the focus of the final author (or redactor) on the refusal of the people to respond to the prophet who speaks the word of God or the prophet's own failure to communicate the word of God to them? Or do we find here both a refusal to listen and a failure to communicate? In the writings of Paul our quest to answer some of these questions appears to be more attainable, because the apostle authored the book himself (by means of an amanuensis/secretary)[10] and we can discern from some of his letters (e.g., Corinthian correspondence) how his message was received.

On the question of free will and predestination, we have the following texts that seem to support the idea of free choice: Jeremiah 7:31-32; 19:4-5; 44:4-5; cf. Deuteronomy 30:15-20; Isaiah 66:3-4; Ecclesiastes 7:29,[11] although a propensity for choosing the *wrong* way is especially evident in these verses (e.g., Luther, *The Bondage of the Will*).

On predestination, I cited the classic work by B. B. Warfield in the *Dictionary of the Bible* edited by James Hastings in the early twentieth century. The many references cited and discussed by this Calvinist theologian bring to the forefront the preponderance of data on the workings of divine foreknowledge and initiative in biblical literature.[12] For example:

- Psalm 130:16; Isaiah 37:26; 46:1 (יָצַר *yātsar*);

- Isaiah 14:24-27; 19:17; Jeremiah 50:45 (יָעַץ *yāats*);

---

10. Gamble, "Amanuensis," 172-73. Evidence of scribal activity is found in the prophetic books (e.g., סֹפֵר *sōpēr* 2 Kgs 19:2; 2 Chr 34:15-20), but here the prophet is often separated in time from the writing and production of the prophetic book.

11. Cited by Meadors in support of free will, *Hardening of the Heart*, 189. See also Tob 13:6 (turn to God). On the self-limitation of divine knowledge for "creaturely freedom," see Pinnock, "God Limits His Knowledge," 147-51. The issue hearkens back to the debates of 1517-25 between Erasmus and Luther documented in Luther's *Bondage of the Will*. See discussion in Kellenberger, *Die Verstockung Pharaos*, 238-41.

12. Warfield, "PREDESTINATION," 47-63. See my ch. I, n34.

- Proverbs 19:21; Isaiah 14:26; 46:10 (עֵצָה *ētsâ*);

Other Hebrew words are cited in the Warfield article; see also Acts 4:28; Romans 8:29-30; 1 Cor 2:7; Ephesians 1:5,11 (Gk. προορίζω, *proorizō*; Lat. *prædestino*).

In the midst of the formidable data regarding predestination, John S. Feinberg argues for free will within divine causation in this way: "an action is free even if causally determined so long as the causes are non-constraining" (called "soft determinism" or "compatibilism"). Feinberg gives the example of a student who is told by the teacher to leave the class (the cause). He prefers to stay, but the teacher tells him that it is in his best interest to leave. The student then freely decides to do so "without constraint," i.e., without the threat of negative actions from the teacher. "For genuinely free human action is seen as *compatible* with non-constraining sufficient conditions which incline the will decisively in one way or another."[13] In regard to such freedom, it does *not* mean that "no agent ever acts under constraint . . . but only that the basic condition of the will is to act without constraint and thus freely. If, however, the agent is causally determined by constraining causes on a particular occasion" the act on that occasion would not be a free act.[14]

Context will determine the presence or the extent of the constraint on the individual agent. Often times, there is tension in the text as we saw in the case of Pharaoh in Exodus 4–14.[15] Was Pharaoh under any (divine or economic) constraint to refuse the request of Moses to "let my people go"? It is not apparent, despite the announcement by YHWH "I will harden Pharaoh's heart."[16] Rashi (ca. 1100) has speculated that perhaps G-d had "strengthened" Pharaoh's heart[17] (Exod 4:21; 9:12; 10:20;

---

13. Feinberg, "God Ordains All," 24–25. In the same volume, Feinberg's Calvinist assumptions regarding divine sovereignty are challenged by: Reichenbach, "God Limits His Power," 101–24, and Pinnock, "God Limits His Knowledge," 143–62.

14. Quotations from J. S. Feinburg "God Ordains All," 24. See also discussion on the limits of free will, divine freedom, and neurodeterminism in Clayton, Walters, and Fischer, *What's with Free Will?*

15. On the view that God may allow or grant hardness of heart instead of merely causing it, see Tigay, "Tolerative/Permissive Hiphil," 397–414; Margain, "Causatif et toleratif," 23–31. See my ch. I, n81.

16. Exod 4:21, "I will harden" Heb. *ḥāzaq* in the Piel impf. with a future sense; but in LXX *future* active, Gk. *sklērynō* as in 4:4, 14 of LXX. In MT Exod 4:4 *ḥāzaq* in Piel perfect, and v. 14 Piel participle. On the future sphere as willed action in Heb, see GKC § 107m.

17. Rashi cited by Moshe Dann, jpost.com 22:03. See also Munk, *Call of Torah*, 87.

CONCLUSION

11:10; 14:4, and that of Egyptians, v. 17) to endure this long contest of ten plagues with the Creator of the world who would inevitably get glory over the gods of Egypt and thus everyone in Egypt would know that YHWH is the true God (14:4). As stated earlier, all three verbs (ḥāzaq, kābēd, qāshâ) are used in Exodus 7 (vv. 3, 13, 14, 22) to denote a similar meaning of Pharaoh's hardening.[18] In Exodus, however, the adjectival use of ḥāzaq as "strength" or "might" is used primarily of YHWH.[19]

In a statement attributed to Rabbi Yoḥanan who defends the actions of YHWH as a response to Pharaoh's longstanding recalcitrance: "So too with the wicked Pharaoh, since Hashem sent five times to him and he took no notice, G-d then said: 'You have stiffened your neck and hardened your heart'" (Exod. R. 13.3).[20]

In his examination of two Greek plays by Sophocles, *Antigone*, and *Oedipus Rex*, Dan Via makes an observation that provides some rationale for Pharaoh's resolute stance:

> In the plays that I'm using as models of the tragic, the blindness of finitude causes noble and aristocratic characters to pursue genuinely valuable goals in such an inordinate and unmoderated way that they cause great harm and suffering to themselves and to others.[21]

The situation of Pharaoh in Exodus may also be included here. Pharaoh too is noble and aristocratic, and he pursues a goal valuable to him (to resume his slave labor projects) in such an inordinate and unmoderated way (*hubris*) that it causes great harm to himself and his Egyptian people. Furthermore, he is blinded by his inability to control the situation that is clearly under YHWH's sovereign rule (his *nemesis*).

God gave Pharaoh a "strong heart" in a more positive sense, see e.g., Qal of חָזַק ḥāzaq, Deut 31:7, 33; Josh 23:6; Piel of חָזַק ḥāzaq, Deut 1:38; 3:28), in *HALOT*, 302–3. The editors of *HALOT* still retain the negative use of חָזַק ḥāzaq ("hardened") with regard to Pharaoh and the Egyptians in Exodus 4–14 and attribute positive attribute only to YHWH.

18. Steinmann, "Hardness of Heart," 381.

19. Dozeman, *Exodus*, 138–39. In the Song Moses and Israel (Exod 15:2): the Lord is my "strength" employs עֹז (ʿōz).

20. https://www.sefaria.org/Shemot_Rabbah.13.3. Erasmus shared a similar view of Pharaoh's initial resistance to God, in his arguments with Luther, 1517–25, *Bondage of the Will*, 20–8.

21. Via, *Tragic Finitude*, 7. Antigone must bury her rebel brother despite Creon's prohibition. Oedipus must find the killer of his royal predecessor at all costs. Via's understanding of finitude is derived from Ricoeur, *Symbolism of Evil*.

Whether one explains the tension between free will and predestination in terms of source-critical considerations (JE, P) or as dramatic tension in the narrative's final form, the tension remains unresolved. In the rabbinic Mishnah Pirkei Avot 3:15a (ca. 200 CE), citing Rabbi Akivah, we read: "Everything is foreseen and free choice is given" (Heb. *hakkōl tzāphûi wəhārshût nətûnâ* הַכֹּל צָפוּי וְהָרְשׁוּת נְתוּנָה).²² Perhaps, in agreement with the R. Akiva quotation, a certain tension should be acknowledge and retained. Are we dealing here with the risky *gift* of free will?

It is appropriate here to discuss the metaphorical language of hardness of heart. What comes to mind is the heart of stone: "I will give you a new heart and put a new spirit in you; I will remove from you your heart of stone (Heb. *et-lēb hāeben* אֶת־לֵב הָאֶבֶן) and give you a heart of flesh" (Ezek 36:26; cf. 11:19). This "heart of stone" (LXX Gk. *tēn kardian tēn lithinēn* τὴν καρδίαν τὴν λιθίνην) is a petrified, inanimate image (3:7–8) in contrast to the animate, living "heart of flesh" (Heb. *lēb bāsār* לֵב בָּשָׂר; Gk. *kardian sarinēn* καρδίαν σαρκίνην).²³ The transplanted heart of flesh is a receptive heart (Jer 32:41; Ezek 3:10). It is "finely attuned to its world and receptive to the divine activity working in and through that world."²⁴

The fossilized, inanimate heart ("heart of stone"; Ezek 36:26; cf. 11:19) also recalls idols of stone and wood (Lev 26:1; Deut 29:17) which "have eyes, but do not see" and "ears but do not hear" and "those who make them are like them" (quotes from Pss 115:4–8; 135:15–18; see also Isa 44:9, 18; Jer 51:17–18; Wis 15:15; Ep Jer 6:64). They who serve these foreign gods are blinded and deaf with a "stubborn and rebellious heart" (Jer 5:19–23; Ezek 14:3; cf. idol worshippers, 1 En. 99:8–9; gentile idolators, Jub. 22:17–18).²⁵ There is a certain whimsical irony in the comparison of the idols made by idol makers (which cannot see or hear) with those who "ascribe worth" to idols (who become spiritually blind and deaf).

As I stated earlier, the hardening terminology is metaphorically applied to various parts of the body: the heart (showing disobedience or stubbornness), but also the ears (deaf, failure to listen, Isa 6:10; 59:1; Zech 7:11),

---

22. Trans. from Neusner, *Mishnah*. Eichrodt concurs: "The fundamental postulate of moral freedom is thus found in equal force alongside the religious conviction of God's effective action in all things;" *Theology of the OT* 2:179.

23. Block, *Ezekiel 25–48*, 356.

24. Quotations from Lamm, *Schleiermacher*, 57–58. A "sensitive and responsive heart," Block, *Ezekiel 1–24*, 353.

25. See Meadors, *Hardening of the Heart*, 2–11, 62.

the eyes (lack of perception, Gen 48:10),[26] the face and forehead (lack of response, Jer 5:3; Ezek 2:4; 3:8–9), the neck, shoulder, and back (Exod 34:9; Deut 9:6; *sarar kathēph*, "stubborn shoulder," Zech 7:11; 2 Chr 30:8; Neh 9:16–17, 29, symbols of insubordination, cf. Hos 4:16).[27]

In the New Testament, the hardening terminology, using *some* Old Testament imagery, in different contexts, is metaphorically applied to various parts of the body: the heart (Eph 4:18; Heb 3:8), mind (Rom 1:28; Eph 4:17; Gk. *nous*),[28] the ears (deaf, failure to listen), the eyes (lack of perception, Mark 4:11–12), and the neck.[29] The semantic field of hardening terminology is rich and diverse.

All the various parts of the body relate to the hardness of the heart idea. Each image conveys the idea in its own specific way, e.g., refusal to listen, inability to understand, unreceptivity, insubordination, noncompliance, and disobedience. If the heart is hardened, one does not hear nor see, nor understand, one becomes stiff-necked (Acts 7:51), stubborn and noncompliant.[30] It is a heart far from God (cf. Mark 7:6; Isa 29:13) that is impious, unattuned, narrow-minded, one-sided, and isolated.[31]

---

26. It is a depletion of the senses of hearing and seeing as seen in Isa 6:9–10.

27. This cluster of images, e.g., blindness, deafness, stiffness, covering a range of attitudes, e.g., refusal to listen, inability to understand, irrationality, and rebelliousness, is surveyed in "Harden, Hardness," Ryken, *Biblical Imagery*, 364. Studies of metaphor will help to clarify the figurative language, see, e.g., George Lakoff and Mark Johnson, *Metaphors*. Also, the study of the interrelationship of body, movement, affect, and sensation may prove useful in the interpretation of this biblical theme of hardening, see, e.g., Massumi, *Parables for the Virtual*.

28. "Mind," *Nous* νοῦς has no equivalent in the OT, although it is often interchangeable with "heart," *kardia*, καρδία, e.g., in the writings of Paul, see Schnelle, *Human Condition*, 105; Bultmann, *Theology 1*, 221; Taylor, "Humanity," 321, 323.

29. The metaphor of the neck (Hebrew *'ōrep*), the part of the animal body that connects the head to the backbone, is taken from the draft animal, whose efforts to resist are localized in the neck, σκληροκαρδία, σκληρός. Spicq and Ernest, *Theological Lexicon* 3, 260. See Ps 105:18 "his neck was put in a collar of iron." "Neck" here in MT is *nephesh*, and in Ps 104:18 LXX *psyche*, elsewhere translated "soul." In LXX Exod 33:5, after the golden calf debacle: "And the Lord said to the sons of Israel, 'you are a stiff-necked (*sklērotrachēlos*) people.'" Earlier in v. 3, the Lord in anger refers to them as "stiff-necked."

30. Acts 7:51 "stubborn and obstinate in your thinking and understanding," Louw and Nida, *Lexicon*, 765. Stephen's indicting address also includes "you ... uncircumcised in hearts and ears" (7:51), using metaphorical language of the LXX (Deut 10:16; 30:6; Jer 4:4; 6:10; 9:25), Beale and Carson, *Commentary*, 569.

31. Last sentence from Lamm, *Schleiermacher*, 96n203, 243, 247 (scattered refs. to the impious heart). Although the introspective self is a modernist notion (e.g., Taylor, *Sources of the Self*) Schleiermacher's insights on the heart resonate with certain biblical texts. See,

The behaviors of those who reject God's prophets and preachers are similar to ideologues, blind partisan advocates of a particular ideology.[32] They rarely listen to reasoned argument and facts that run contrary to their views. They will keep their ideology even if it may kill them or others (e.g., in acts of conquest) because they have invested too much in it. The ideology could reflect, for example, idolatry, domination, parochialism, exploitation. In the case of the kings, it might be hubris, stubbornly maintaining their ill-fated policies (Israelite slave labor, futile wars, misguided alliances). In the case of the people, the embrace of an ideology might be a defense mechanism[33] to legitimize a divided allegiance, whether its YHWH and Asherah, the king and his treaties, God and Mammon, Jerusalem and Rome, profession and practice.[34] Literary and historical contexts inform what type of ideology is embraced and what may have prompted it. This query may provide another motive or reason behind the stubborn, uncooperative, noncompliance that I have labeled: hardness of heart.

In the commission of Isaiah 6:9-10, is the hardening of his audience here a "compensation" for some "deficiency" in communication and compliance?[35] From what I can discern from the diverse sources (2 Kgs 16:1-2, 5-7; 2 Chr 28:1-6), King Ahaz and the people (Isa 7:2, 17) were not compliant regarding the prophet's message. The hardening statement in Isaiah's commission (vv. 9-10) therefore seems to function *for the prophet* in this compensatory way, supporting Isaiah 6 as a literary memoir (see my ch. I, nn53-54).

The same Isaianic statement is situated in the ministry of Jesus (according to Luke 8:9-10; para. Matt 13:10-17; Mark 4:10-12) as well as in the mission of Paul at Rome (according to Acts 28:26-28). In the last passage, the author of Acts sees it as a climactic conclusion that began at Pisidian

---

e.g., Jer 5:23; Ezek 3:7; 14:3; 20:16.

32. See my ch. I, n64.

33. On defense mechanism, see https://www.psychologytoday.com/us/basics/defense-mechanisms#10-major-defense-mechanisms.

34. As mentioned in my introduction regarding Kierkegaard and the purity of heart (Matt 5:8), I cited the double-minded ("two-souled" *dipsychos* δίψυχος) in James 1:8; 4:8; the double heart in Psalm 12:2; Sirach 1:28; 1 Enoch 91:4; and by way of illustration, Romans 7:15.

35. Kaplan suggests that Isaiah 6 reflects the prophet's despairing reflection on the failure of his attempts to convince the people to repent, written after he had been active for some time, in his "Isaiah 6:1-11," 251-59. For an example of compensatory behaviors, see Jung, "Unconscious," 50-51.

Antioch (Acts 13:44-47) and continued at Corinth (18:5) and Ephesus (19:8-9) before a final *pronouncement* in Rome.[36] Such a pronouncement has a "performative function" on the addressees as we have seen earlier in Israel's prophets.[37] What is the motivation of the pronouncement by the addresser? Is it a self-fulfilling word from God (cf. Jer 1:12; 4:28)?[38] Can the prophecy of hardening also function here in a compensatory manner to account for the noncompliance of so many Judeans?

If we understand the pronouncements in Luke 8:10 and Acts 28:26-28 as compensatory, were they conscious or unconscious contrivances? In Acts 27:27 an angel appeared at night (in a dream?) to Paul the prisoner stating that he would "stand before Caesar." Nevertheless, the author of Acts makes it evident that the hardening of the Jews/Judeans leading to a mission to the gentiles seems to be a conscious effort on his part, perhaps to compensate for Jewish rejection and to justify the more-receptive gentile mission.

The hardening of Israel in both the Hebrew Bible and the New Testament raises questions about its permanence and the ongoing validity of God's promises to historic Israel (Gen 12:1-3; 15:1-21; 17:1-11; Exod 6:6-8; 19:4-6; Jer 31:31-34; Ezek 36:25-28). In Romans 11:25-26a, Mark Nanos, citing ancient medical texts (e.g., Hippocrates, *De Fractures* 23.10; *De Articulus* 15.6; Galen, *Ars Medica* 1.387; Celsus, *De Medicina*), argues that "a protective callus has formed on Israel" until the full number of the gentiles comes in, "then all Israel will be healed."[39] In my previous chapter on the Old Testament, I had shown that hardness of heart carries a broad and diverse set of meanings, as for example, in Isaiah 6:10 where "fat heart" (Heb. שָׁמֵן *shāmēn*; 1QIsa^a) speaks of a slow, languid, self-oriented set of responses, incapable of decisive, self-sacrificial action.[40] Certainly the meanings of the

---

36. Luke shortens his quotation of Isaiah 6:9-10 in Luke 8, so that it is significantly shorter than what Matthew and Mark have. What is the reason for this redaction? Perhaps Luke is saving the full hardening statement of Isaiah 6:9-10 for the very conclusion of Acts. For a more complete explanation of the mission to the gentiles in Luke-Acts, see Puskas, *Conclusion*, 4-6, 125-31.

37. See speech-act theory in *Thiselton on Hermeneutics*, 61-66, 84-86, citing the works of, e.g., J. L. Austin and J. R. Seale. As with the prophetic word of judgment or salvation, the blessing or the curse, the hardening pronouncement has a performative effect on its listeners. See also my ch. I, n50 and ch. II, nn54-55.

38. Phrase and citations from Lundbom, "Jeremiah," 718.

39. In Nanos, *Reading Romans 2*, 153-78. Dunn also includes as an optional rendering of *pōrōsis* "a callus which unites a fractured bone," *Romans 9-16*, 640.

40. Oswalt, *Isaiah, Chapters 1-39*, 189n10; see also Gerstenberger, *Psalms*, 184.

early Christian language of "hardening" could also convey the broad and diverse set of meanings, in different contexts and ways.[41]

In Romans 11:25–29 (cf. 15:9–13; ca. 57 CE), Joel Kaminsky and Mark Reasoner argue that the statement "all Israel will be saved" includes the historic people of Israel along with Messiah-believers, in response to N. T. Wright's redefinition of "all Israel" as comprised only of Messiah-believing gentiles and Jews.[42] I discuss this matter more carefully in my appendix: "On Natural and Grafted Branches (Romans 11:17–24): Israel and the Church in Robert Jenson's *Systematic Theology*,[43] Ancillary or Necessary Concern?" The appendix has important implications for questions regarding the hardening of historic Israel and the church's place in God's salvation history. In my appendix, you will see that the metaphor of the olive tree with "bent" branches and new branches grafted into the tree (11:17–24) are textually linked by Paul with his discussion of "the hardening of Israel" (11:25–26).

---

41. I am merely showing here that the fluidity of meanings has a history, and not assuming that the semantic value of OT hardening words can be immediately transferred to the NT without recognizing different contexts, see *Thiselton on Hermeneutics* (2006), discussing James Barr's criticism of certain articles in *TDNT*: One cannot "lump together the meaning of words drawn from various different contexts, and 'expound' them as the meaning of the word in a given verse." Ibid, 201.

42. Kaminsky and Reasoner, "Israel's Election," 446. See Wright, *Paul and Faithfulness*, 1244–45.

I should mention here that Rom 9:6–8 concerns a comparison of biological children (historic Israel) and spiritual heirs (faithful Jews and gentiles). In Galatians 3–4, Paul makes his case for *gentiles* to become children of promise without adhering to the Jewish observance of the law. See 1 Corinthians 9:20, where he does not condemn those who are "under the law." See also Paul's statements on the law and commandments as "holy, righteous, and good" (Rom 7:12), faith working through love (Gal 5:6; Rom 1:5), and love fulfilling the law (Rom 13:9–10).

43. Jenson, *Systematic Theology: Vols. 1 and 2*.

APPENDIX

On Natural and Grafted Branches (Romans 11:17–24)

Israel and the Church in Robert Jenson's *Systematic Theology*,[1] Ancillary or Necessary Concern?

THERE ARE MANY WAYS to analyze and address Israel and the church, especially as it concerns those who identify with the faith of Israel in the Jewish Scriptures and those who would identify with the followers of Christ in the New Testament. It is for this reason that I decided to examine the work of a Christian theologian here who has responded to the issue with sensitivity and sincere concern. I cite New Testament scholar, N. T. Wright's definition of theology to substantiate this inclusion: "theology suggests certain ways of telling the story, explores certain ways of answering the questions, offers particular interpretations of the symbols, and suggests and critiques certain forms of praxis."[2] Theologian, Karl Barth, reminds us, "the dogmatician has also an exegetical and the exegete a dogmatic responsibility."[3]

In this appendix, I will tell the story of Israel and the church addressing key questions, interpreting its symbols, and providing a critique of certain

---

1. Jenson, *Systematic Theology: Vols 1* and *2*. Extensive ref. to this two-volume work will be indicated by vol. and page number, e.g., *ST* 2:193.

2. Wright, *People of God*, 126. I do not agree, however, with Wright's interpretation of Romans 11:26, "all Israel," as excluding Jews who are not Christ followers in a reconfigured people of God, *Paul and Faithfulness*, 1244–45. See my ch. II, nn23, 36.

3. Barth, *Church Dogmatics III/2*, ix.

forms of praxis. It is my hope that it will lead to a "more positive Christian theology of Judaism or a more positive Jewish theology of Christianity."[4]

In my reading of Jenson's theology, I noticed sympathetic discussion of Israel and the church, with special reference to Romans 11, occurring in key sections of his two-volume work. It raised a question for me: How necessary is it for a systematic theology that purports to be ecumenical to also include a special place for Israel and Jewish thought? First, I will address the related question: why we should *expect* such discussion in a systematic theology? Next, I will review some recent discussion on this theme. Then, I will locate Jenson's statements on Israel and the church under *the grid* of another ecumenical theologian engaged in the same concern. I will also survey some research on Israel in Romans 11, look at some of Jenson's Jewish dialogue partners, and finally, his comments on "our biblical heritage."

As I mentioned, in reading of Jenson's *Systematic Theology*, I came upon the question that drives this study (ancillary or necessary?) after encountering statements like: Supersessionism "must be and is being overcome" (*ST* 2:193, cf. 335). "Members of Israel according to the flesh, whatever else can be said about them, do not need to be grafted into God's olive tree" (*ST* 2:363).[5] "No child of Abraham will be excluded because she or he is not baptized" (*ST* 2:363). References to Israel and the church, especially to Romans 11, are mentioned several times in Jenson's *Systematic Theology* (*ST* 2:191, 335, 361) and elsewhere by him (e.g., Braaten and Jenson, *Jews & Christians: People of God*, 4–5).

In Jenson's two-volume *Systematic Theology*, these statements I just mentioned are located in his discussions of (1) the church's use of the canon of Israel's Scripture (1:30),[6] (2) the Triune identity of Israel's God, whom Je-

---

4. Quote from Jewish scholar David Novak, "Theology and Philosophy," 97. See also in this Appx., p. 66.

5. On "Israel according to the flesh": Historic Israel is probably meant here (cf. Heb 7:16) as distinguished from the "new arrivals" that are grafted in. Romans 11:23 states that "they ('Israel' not in Gk. here) will be *grafted in*, for God has power to *graft them in again*" and in v. 24 "how much more will these natural branches (historic Israel) be *grafted back into* their own olive tree," which is much easier to do with branches from *the same* tree! (parentheses and *italics* are my comments). Perhaps the emphasis in Jenson's statement above (*ST* 2:363) is on "do not *need* to be grafted into." See also in this Appendix, n43 where I discuss the work of Jewish scholar Mark Nanos, who argues that the olive tree branches are "bent" but *not* broken off (Rom 11:17–20), http://www.marknanos.com/.

6. Are Jews today in a much less favorable position to comprehend the meaning of God's redemptive love in Scripture than are the Christians? Cannot both have an

APPENDIX: ON NATURAL AND GRAFTED BRANCHES

sus called Father (1:42-53, 75-80),[7] (3) Augustine's *totus Christus* and *totus puer domini* (1:80-84),[8] (4) Torah and gospel (1:230-31), (5) Israel and the nations (2:170-71),[9] (6) the church as an event within Israel (2:182-83), (7) Israel and the church as the people of God (2:190-95), (8) Judaism as a continuation of Israel (2:334-36), and (9) the salvation of all Israel (2:360-64).[10] All of these points are relevant to the discussion of the hardening of historic Israel and the inclusion of the church in God's salvation history.

It was surprising to me, at least, that a Trinitarian theologian of Norwegian descent, raised on Luther's Catechism, and educated at Germany's renowned Heidelberg University, would be so forthright about Israel and her descendants "after the flesh" (historic Israel). So I then asked: is it presented as an ancillary, incidental topos, or something necessary and vital to his theological enterprise? Also, should it be a mere appendage or an integral part of Christian theology?

Some of us may be surprised at Jenson's respect for Israel and her natural descendants. Was he not raised on the teaching of Martin Luther? What about Luther's 1543 treatise "On the Jews and their Lies" (*LW* 47:137-306)? It was championed by xenophobes in the "anti-Semitism Controversy" of Bismarck's Germany (1881) and later, by the Nazis.[11] Did

---

immediate and direct claim as a "continuation of canonical Israel?" (*ST* 1:30n23).

7. Cunningham, "Israel's Covenantal Life," 196.

8. Jenson uses *totus Christus* to explain the relationship of Christ to his church (2:173, 175). Although he provides only two quotes from Augustine to support his use of *totus Christus* ("the risen Christ including and included in his community") and his derivative *totus puer domini* ("a total servant of the Lord," *ST1*, 81, 83, 85-86).

9. I have not found the issue of Israeli Zionism discussed in Jenson's *Systematic Theology*, but a case can be made that one can be a critic of current Israeli policies toward Palestinians without being anti-Jewish or anti-Semitic, see my discussion in this Appxdix, n47.

10. Wright interprets "all Israel" in Rom 11:26 to refer to a "spiritual Israel," a reconfigured people of God, i.e., the church, and he cites some church fathers for his support, *Climax*, 250. For other interpretations, see my chs. II, nn23, 36, and my Appendix, n41. Upon the death of Mattathias, father of Judas Maccabeus, "all Israel" mourned for him (1 Macc 2:70, cf. Mark 1:33). Our study, however, which concerns God's action on behalf of "all Israel" should not be discounted as mere hyperbole.

11. Gritsch, *Luther's Anti-Semitism*, 111, 115. See also an earlier sermon "That Jesus Christ was Born a Jew" 1523 by Luther (a scholar of the Hebrew Scriptures), *LW* 45:200-201,229. It has some constructive points, e.g., "If one is to boast of flesh and blood, the Jews are actually nearer to Christ than we are, as St. Paul says in Romans 9[:5]." Much of it, though, discounts the Jewish interpretation of biblical passages that Christians use to defend the messiahship of Jesus (Gen 3:15; 49:10f; Isa 7:14; Dan

Jenson not study at the University of Heidelberg? I do not wish to slight Germany's world-famous university, with its history of outstanding faculty (e.g., Hegel, Feuerbach, Troeltsch, Weber, Von Rad, Jaspers, Gadamer, Westermann), but when Jenson was a student there it was only twelve years after the infamous Third Reich, when the University of Heidelberg had purged all its Jewish faculty and adopted Nazi ideology in its curriculum.[12] This regime, as we know, was responsible for the murder of millions of Jews (including, gypsies, socialists, etc.). Jewish philosopher, Hannah Arendt, a Heidelberg alumna, had barely escaped arrest herself.

Some Recent Discussion on the Topic

For German scholars complicit in anti-Semitism during this tyrannical period, see Robert P. Ericksen, *Theologians under Hitler: Gerhard Kittel, Paul Althaus and Emmanuel Hirsch*; Paul R. Hinlicky, *Before Auschwitz: What Christian Theology Must Learn from the Rise of Nazism*; and Susannah Heschel, *The Aryan Jesus: Christian Theologians and the Bible in Nazi Germany*. A common theme in the above titles, is that these German theologians (mistakenly) believed that they were pursuing or advocating a moderate course of action (e.g., tolerating Jewish ghettoization), which merely underscores how extreme and violent was the anti-Semitism under the Third Reich.[13]

Some of us may be familiar with titles on Jewish-Christian dialogue (e.g., by Charlotte Klein, Paul Van Buren, and especially R. Kendall Soulen),[14] the closely related titles on the importance of doing respon-

---

9:24ff). Luther's attacks, in his 1543 treatise, may have been addressed to observant Jews who *bested* him in theological debates regarding the Torah.

12. Not unlike all German universities under Hitler's Third Reich, Heidelberg was tainted by this period of overt anti-Semitism. For example, in 1936, Heidelberg University officials protested President Nicholas M. Butler's selection of a *Jewish* delegate to represent Columbia University at Heidelberg's 550th anniversary celebration, Butler replied that at Columbia, delegates were selected on the basis of merit, not *race*. Many students were *outraged* that President Butler had even *accepted* Heidelberg's invitation at all. As it was, however, Heidelberg had already purged its Jewish professors and adopted *Nazi ideology* in its curriculum, see Rosenthal, *Nicholas Butler*. On Hannah Arendt's narrow escape from the Gestapo, see Maier-Katkin, *Stranger from Abroad*, 81–83.

13. See also McGovern and Sait, *From Luther to Hitler*, and the following work which attempts to remove any causal connection between Luther and Nazi ideology, such as Siemon-Netto, *Fabricated Luther*.

14. The works of Soulen and Van Buren are cited in Jenson, *ST* 2, 193n. 29. Jenson

sible theology in the post-holocaust (post-Shoah) era (e.g., Richard L. Rubenstein, Michael L. Morgan),[15] and have read or heard of church statements like *Nostra Aetate* (Vatican II) and Pope John Paul II's "Address at the Great Synagogue in Rome" April 13, 1986.[16] It may be appropriate to mention here that events of the last century involving the church and Judaism make it necessary for every Christian theologian to be concerned about Israel and Judaism in a genuine dialogue *that is not merely patronizing* or an "antiphonal monologue."[17]

Why should a Christian theology, like Jenson's work, be so concerned about supersessionism with regard to Judaism? In addition to the history of anti-Semitism mentioned above, the assessment of Jewish philosopher David Novak is noteworthy. Writing on supersessionism in the chapter of a book edited by Braaten and Jenson, *Jews and Christians: People of God*,[18] Novak makes the following observation. Learned Jews confronted by Christian supersessionism often react with their own version of counter-supersessionism. They respond "that Christians are a group of gentiles who erroneously—even arrogantly—think they are now God's people exclusively, having been first led to this position by a group of renegade Jews who removed themselves from Judaism . . . (they) do not worship the Lord God of Israel as do the Jews, but rather, another god altogether."[19] Novak adds that "the logic of this Jewish rejection of Christianity runs parallel to the logic of Christian supersessionism."[20] It is interesting that the "Institute

---

also cites the following title, Klein *Anti-Judaism in Theology*.

15. Morgan, *Holocaust Reader*; Rubenstein, *After Auschwitz*.

16. On relations to non-Christian religions in (opening phrase) "our age," *Nostra Aetate*, see *Docs. Vatican II*. Regarding the 1998 address by Pope John Paul II "We Remember," Heschel takes issue with his attempt to *distinguish* Christian theological anti-Judaism from anti-Semitism, citing the research of Uriel Tal (on the religious and non-religious roots of anti-Semitism), in her *Aryan Jesus*, 20–21, 323.

17. Novak, "Theology and Philosophy," 43. Karma Ben-Johanan reexamines Judaism in Catholic theology and Christianity in Orthodox Judaism, in *Jacob's Younger Brother*.

18. Novak, "From Supersessionism to Parallelism," 95–113.

19. Novak, "From Supersessionism to Parallelism," 96. This Jewish caricature of Christianity ("another god") is not too dissimilar from that advocated by Marcion of Sinope, in Pontus (ca., 150 CE) who taught that the OT god was an evil/deceptive creator (or demiurge) and not the loving Father of Jesus Christ. He thus rejected the OT and accepted only certain NT books that were not "Jewish," i.e., some of Paul's letters and an edited version of Luke's Gospel. See Harnack, *Marcion*, 15–24; BeDuhn, *Marcion's Canon*, 20–33.

20. Novak, "From Supersessionism to Parallelism," 96. Jon Levenson's *Death and*

for the Study and Eradication of Jewish Influence on German Church Life" (1939–42) of the *Reichskirche* (*Deutsche Evangelische Kirche*, 1933–45) described by Susannah Heschel, in *The Aryan Jesus: Christian Theologians and the Bible in Nazi Germany* (Princeton, 2008), chaps. 2–3, mirrors the Marcionite image of Christianity portrayed in the Jewish counter-supersessionism mentioned above by Novak.[21] He concludes that the "renunciation of supersessionism as either thesis or antithesis is the necessary precondition both for a more positive Christian theology of Judaism and a more positive Jewish theology of Christianity."[22] Therefore, I will show that it is necessary for a systematic theology that intends to be ecumenical, like Jensons's work, to include a place for Israel and subsequent Jewish thought, not as an appendage but as an integral part of the work.

Locating Jenson's Statements Using a Grid (provided by R. Kendall Soulen)

How does Jenson make his case for Israel and the church as a necessary *topos* of systematic theology? In an article, "(*ha-Shem*) YHWH The Triune God," R. Kendall Soulen, whose earlier work is cited favorably by Jenson, presents several helpful theses related to our discussion: (1) (*ha-Shem*) YHWH the triune God is the God revealed in the gospel, (2) "*that fidelity to the gospel requires rejection of supersessionism*" and also (3) "*the affirmation of God's unbroken faithfulness to God's covenant with the people Israel.*"[23] In

---

Resurrection contends that Christians learned supersessionism from the Jews who saw themselves as superseding the nations. For examples of supersessionism in European biblical scholarship on Luke-Acts, see "Christianity as the true faith of Israel," 7, n14 and "the hardening of Israel as a group," 23, n61, in my revised dissertation, Puskas, *Conclusion*. On these related themes (above), I read some of these European authors on Judaism (e.g., Loisy, Weiss, Holtzmann, Conzelmann, Haenchen) to my wife, Susan, who is of Jewish ancestry, and she found them offensive.

21. "Only a Marcionite—who is the reduction ad absurdum of supersessionism—could posit that God's promise to the church comes ex nihilo and thus presuppose nothing before it." Novak, "From Supersessionism to Parallelism," 99.

22. Novak, "From Supersessionism to Parallelism," 97. See Salmon, *Preaching without Contempt*, which heightens awareness of the problem with helpful suggestions to avoid it in a manner that is sensitive to those who are less astute on the issue. She cites, favorably, the Braaten and Jenson title, *Jews and Christians*, on 37 and 164n1 of her book.

23. Soulen, "YHWH," 44–45. Soulen in the above article, had faulted Jenson, along with Barth, to be "partially satisfying" and "leaves the problem of supersessionism partly addressed," in his "YHWH," 44. However, Soulen cites Jenson's *earlier* work, *The*

APPENDIX: ON NATURAL AND GRAFTED BRANCHES

my reading of Jenson's *Systematic Theology*, I will show that Jenson's work coincides significantly with the above theses of Soulen.

(1) Regarding the Sacred Name (Tetragrammaton) of the God of Israel.

Jenson writes

> Asked about her access to this God, Israel's answer is, "we are permitted to call him by name"—just so, the name was eventually felt too holy for regular utterance aloud and was replaced by stated euphemisms, in reading Scripture by *Adonai*, "The Lord." The name does not thereby lose its power, on the contrary, in rabbinic discourse the phrase *Hashem*, "the Name" is often itself used instead of God. (*ST* 1:44)

Jenson adds "the recent fashion of pronouncing the name [JHWH] in lectures and from the pulpit is deeply regrettable" (1:44n12).[24]

Concerning the sacred name (i.e., YHWH or Jenson's more Teutonic JHWH) as the God of the gospel (cf. Soulen), Jenson writes of God "the one who rescued Israel from Egypt" is the one who also "raised the Israelite Jesus from the dead" (1:44). Colleague and friend, Carl E. Braaten cites this phrase, with apparent approval, in his review of Jenson's *Systematic Theology;* so also agrees biblical scholar, Christopher Seitz.[25] Jenson adds "It is the God of Israel whom Jesus called Father and to whom the disciples wanted to pray" (1:42).[26] Regarding the Holy Spirit, he writes "we should no more want to specify an identity of the Spirit without reference to Israel and the church . . . than we

Triune Identity, stating in an endnote that "Jenson has published a more recent trinitarian theology, *The Triune God*, vol. 1 of *Systematic Theology* (Oxford: Oxford University Press, 1997), which may not be vulnerable to the same criticism made here," in Soulen, "YHWH," 53, n33. Jenson has also noted favorably Soulen's magnum opus, *God of Israel* in his *ST* 2:193, n29, describing Soulen's book as "the most sustained and properly theological investigation of this matter." Jewish scholar, David Novak, expresses similar positive sentiments regarding Soulen's book, "Supersessionism to Parallelism," 95, n1.

24. The use of JHWH is a significant improvement from Jenson's use of "Jahve" in his 1973 title, *Story and Promise*, 41. I prefer YHWH, see my Intro., n9.

25. Braaten, "Eschatology and Mission,"303, and Seitz, "Handing Over the Name," 23–24, both in Gunton, *Trinity, Time and Church*.

26. Luther concedes that the Jews (along with the Turks, etc.) "believe in and worship only the one, true God" nevertheless he concludes that "they do not know what his [God's] attitude is toward them." *Large Catechism*, in *Book of Concord*, 440.66. [brackets] are mine.

would want to specify an identity of the Son without Jesus" (1:148) and later of the Spirit "he is the *ruach* of the God of Israel" (1:160). In Jenson's discussion of the theological problem, he writes "the Father is to be addressed as the God of Israel and that the Trinity is the God of Israel" (1:122) which for Jenson is "a plain phenomenon of the gospel's narrative" (1:124). More will be mentioned of Israel and the Triune One.

Why did not the early church return to uttering *HaShem* for JHWH or its oral substitute *Adonai*? Jenson replies:

> A new kind of naming also appears . . . the gospel's messengers must again name the God to whom they introduce hearers. They do not return to uttering (the sacred name) "JHWH." Instead they name the one whom God had raised and identify God by constructions that incorporate this naming.[27]

(2) "fidelity to the gospel requires rejection of supersessionism"

Jenson states that supersessionism—the idea "that the church succeeds Israel in such a fashion as to *displace* from the status of God's people those Jews who do not enter the church"—"must be and is being overcome" (*ST* 2:193, cf. 335).[28] Yet Jenson is quick to point out that "developing a less Trinitarian Christology is precisely how *not* to repent of supersessionsim."[29]

---

27. *ST* 1:44-45. On 45, n20, Jenson adds "As a name, *kyrios* appears in the New Testament only in reference to Hebrew Scripture, where it translates *adonai*, the cover Israel had adopted for purposes of public utterance." Why was *kyrios* in the Greek Septuagint a translation of the Hebrew Tetragrammaton (YHWH)? Because as early as the third century BCE (when the LXX translation began) YHWH was pronounced *adonai* ("Lord") to avoid pronouncing the sacred name. See also Seitz, "Handing Over the Name," 31-32 in Gunton, *Trinity, Time, and Church*, where he cites several places where the NT associates the divine name YHWH (Gk. *kyrios*) with Jesus.

28. "Jews" in the NT (Gk., *Ioudiaoi*), refers to Judeans of the Israelite faith (e.g., Josephus, *Antiq*. 11.173). The region of Judea is also the location of Jerusalem where some standard of Israelite faith was established with the second temple, see Malina and Pilch, *Social Science*, 372. There are contexts, however, where the religious (or cultural) term, "Jews" is preferred over the ethnic-geographical "Judean" (Josephus, *Antiq*. 20.38-39; 2 Macc 6:6) cited in Levine, *Misunderstood Jew*, 161-62. There are also modern Jewish concerns about too readily replacing "Jews" with "Judeans" in the NT as a subtle (anti-Semitic?) attempt to *undermine* any sense of continuity in Jewish history, Joshua D. Garroway, "*Ioudiaos*" 524-25. Nevertheless, Cohen, supports "Judean" (ethnic-geographical) over "Jew" (religious term) for "*Ioudaios*" in the NT, *EDEJ* 769-70. See also my ch. II, n27.

29. *ST* 2:193n.29. In his Trinitarian Christology, Jenson appeals to *totus Christus* ("the risen Christ including and included in his community" from Augustine) and for

From my reading of Jenson, he would have little problem with the following statement by Philip A. Cunningham:

> With the Triune One in mind, Christians can understand God's calling the people of Israel into being as a covenantal community as an experience of God's creative power, as an invitation to enter into permanent relationship, and as empowerment to become a unique people. The Logos and Spirit have been involved in Israel's covenantal life since its inception. Christians, for example, understand the Torah as an expression of the Word of God, and the Nicene Creed confesses that the Holy Spirit "has spoken through the prophets."[30]

R. Kendall Soulen, who is a contributor to *Jews and Christians: People of God* (eds., Braaten and Jenson), concludes his study:

> The New Testament uses an astonishing array of periphrastic language to identify the one to whom Jesus prays as (*haShem*) YHWH, the God of Israel, and in order to include Jesus and the Spirit in the identity of this one God.[31]

Regarding Jesus as the fulfiller of Israel's promises, Jenson does not suppose that the problem of supersessionism will be overcome by *forsaking* a "belief that the advent of Jesus Christ definitely fulfills the promises of Israel" (2:335).[32] Jenson firmly maintains these Christological convictions, while conceding that:

Israel and the Isaianic Servant Songs *totus puer domini* ("a total servant of the Lord,") ST 1:81, 83, 85–86; see also 2:173, 175. Here the agent is identified *within* but is also *above* the community. The concept is not unlike that of, e.g., "corporate personality" or "corporate solidarity" ("the one for the many") as in Isa 53; Acts 9:4; 22:7; 26:14 where Christ/his people are persecuted by Saul, see H. Wheeler Robinson, *Corporate Personality in Ancient Israel*. See also my ch. I, n54. For purposes of Jewish-Christian dialogue, the concepts of *totus puer domini* (related to *totus Christus* above) or even corporate solidarity or corporate personality are preferable to the distinctly Christian *totus Christus*.

30. Philip A. Cunningham, "The Triune One, the Incarnate Logos, and Israel's Covenantal Life," in Cunningham et al., *Christ Jesus and the Jewish People Today* (2011), 196. On Jenson regarding the Triune God and Israel, see ST 1: 42–44, 115, 122, 124, 148, 160.

31. Soulen, "Tetragrammaton and Trinity" 27.

32. Jenson cites an article by Soulen, commenting that it is "otherwise very helpful" although "slightly bent by this assumption" (that Barth who saw Christ as the *fulfillment* of Israel's promises did *not* correctly understand how it could also *lead to* an *unfair elevation of the church* superseding Judaism as the new and true people of God), see Soulen, "Karl Barth and the Future," 413–28.

APPENDIX: ON NATURAL AND GRAFTED BRANCHES

> In the time of the church until the time of Judgment, the Judaism of Israel according to the flesh must continue . . . precisely because Israel did not believe, . . . lest "the gifts and the calling of God" prove after all revocable. And since the church is doomed to be mostly gentile, this Judaism must continue lest God's *torah* be forgotten. For within the perfected polity of God it will eternally be the role of the one hundred and forty-four thousand to remember every one of God's commands and lead in the praise of God for them. (*ST* 2:336)

In a paradoxical note on the above quote (2:336, n85) Jenson points out that to deny "Judaism's defining disbelief in Jesus' Resurrection" as regrettable as it is, would be to deny Christianity itself. So for Jenson, Christian distinctives are to be maintained alongside the viable and legitimate alternative of Judaism today.

Thus Jenson can affirm "The Jewish way of life did *not* in fact end" (2:193).[33] I mention this phrase later with regard to Jenson's plea for "sober recognition of the history and its present mandate" (2:193). Elsewhere Jenson writes, "Christianity needs a theological interpretation of Judaism, and not a supersessionist one."[34] He concludes "so long as the time of detour lasts, the embodiment of the risen Christ is whole only in the form of the church and an identifiable community of Abraham and Sarah's descendants.[35] The church and the synagogue are together and only together: the present availability to the world of the risen Jesus Christ."[36] This "detour" of which Jenson

---

33. It is on this theme that Jenson cites Soulen, *God of Israel and Christian Theology* as "the most sustained and properly theological investigation of this matter" *ST* 2:193, n29. In Judaism, after the temple's destruction (70 CE), daily prayers "replace" daily temple sacrifice (*b. Ber.* 1a; 28b; *b. Sukk.* 51b) and prayer, repentance, and almsgiving achieve atonement (*b. Sukk.* 49b; *Avot de R. Natan* 4.5). Rabbis, however, point out that the loss of the temple is to be mourned (*Tisha b'Av* fast) and the subsequent transition, inevitably divinely arranged, e.g., a tradition of prayer as the "service of the heart" had *preceded* temple worship (e.g., Gen 18:18–33; 20:17), *few sins required* sacrifice, which were *limited to* the Temple Mount, according to Donin, *To Be a Jew*, 160–61, 264.

34. Jenson, "Theology of Judaism," 6.

35. Jenson, "Theology of Judaism," 13. In his *Systematic Theology*, Jenson adds "Judaism is a continuation of Israel very specifically 'according to the flesh': it understands Israel as the 'children of an original ancestral couple, Abraham and Sarah" (*ST* 2:355), citing in support here Neusner, *Rabbinic Judaism*, 124. It seems clear here that "Israel according to the flesh" is historic Israel which would include the faithful as well as those who wish to belong to it, according to the prophets (Isa 37:31–32; Jer 23:3; 31:7–8; Ezek 11:19–21; Mal 3:16–17).

36. Jenson, "Theology of Judaism," 13. Jenson sees "a person's embodiment" as the

writes is a mutual one created by Christ's advent moving forward both the church and the synagogue in two different but parallel courses. The divided people of God, Jenson mentions, concerns a "divided church" as well as Jews and Christians.[37] For Jenson, it is in the Great Culmination that all schisms shall end, all becoming one with the second advent of Christ. Perhaps it is with this sense of incompleteness regarding a shared journey and destiny of the divided people of God that we can begin to relax the historic tensions surrounding "Israel and the church."

In the same paragraph where Jenson states confidently that "No child of Abraham will be excluded because she or he is not baptized" (*ST* 2:363), he adds with apparent sensitivity to the scandal of particularity and also the matter of the church's acceptance of Jewish Christians "it must also quickly be said that the church must regard the baptism of those Jews whom the Father grants her as a vital element of her own life."[38] These ironic statements are preceded by a discussion of universal affirmations providing a dialectic of God's initiative and the response of faith

> The logic especially of Paul's own soteriology can never stop short of universal affirmations.... Nor can Paul's hope for Israel be supported otherwise than with universals: "And so all Israel will be saved.... For God has imprisoned all in disobedience so that he may be merciful to all" (Rom 11:26-32).[39]

---

necessary means of his or her self-transcending "*availability* to other persons." Here as the body of Christ, the church embodies and makes available to others the risen Christ. *ST* 2:213-15. See also by Jenson, *Essays*, 219-21.

37. Lamenting that a theology of a "unique and unitary church of the creeds," is no longer possible, Jenson concludes "To live as the church in the situation of a divided church — if that can happen at all — must at least mean that we live in radical self-contradiction and that by every churchly act we contradict that contradiction. Also theology must make this double contradiction at and by every step of its way." *ST* 1:vii.

38. Jenson also cites in a note his discussion of John's Gospel on the matter of faith in the Son who is one with the Father, *ST* 2:71. An appeal to *totus puer domini* and *totus Christus* (1:81-86), may be appropriate here in response to this *challenge* of particularity (Acts 4:11-12) and to maintain a détente in Jewish-Christian dialogue. I cite here also the works by the famous cardinal (of Jewish ancestry), Lustiger, *Christians and Jews*.

39. *ST* 2:361. I should mention here that Rom 9:27-29 and 11:1-5 concern remnant theology as advocated by the prophets (after judgment, Amos 5:15; 9:12; Mic 4:7; surviving the Assyrian invasion, Isa 10-11; survivors of nations, Amos 1:8; 9:1-2; Isa 10:19; Israel returning from exile, Isa 46:3-4; Jer 23:3; 31:7-8; Ezek 9:8; 11:13, 19-21; 39:28; including gentiles, Isa 66:20-21): it is a divine action, Mal 3:16-18; of rescue, Rom 9:27; by God's grace, 11:5, see my ch. I, n105.

Jenson's quotation here has similarities with what Jon Levenson writes about in his essay, "The Universal Horizon of Biblical Particularism." Levenson reexamines the issues of universalism (God's availability to the world, e.g., Isa 56:6–8) and particularity (Israel as God's chosen people, Exod 19:6). He argues that both Judaism and Christianity (citing Gal 3:36–39) must remain true to their foundational literature (and their interpretation of it), which for each underscores the basis of its own existence.[40] Only in this way, all Israel, as historic Israel, will be saved.

(3) "Concerning God's unbroken faithfulness to God's covenant[41] with Israel,"

Citing Romans 11:26, 29, Jenson writes "Paul was sure, if of anything, that 'the calling of God' is 'irrevocable.' [that Paul is] Compelled to believe that 'all Israel'... must somehow finally be saved" (*ST* 2:335).[42] Jenson adds that "Members of Israel according to the flesh, whatever else can be said about them, do not need to be grafted into God's olive tree" (*ST* 2:363). Actually, Paul does mention in Romans 11:23 that "those of Israel ['Israel' not in Gk.] will be *grafted in*, for God has power to *graft them in again*" and in v. 24

---

40. Levenson, *Ethnicity and the Bible*, 143–69. See also by Levenson "Did God Forgive Adam? 148-70. It compares Rom 5:12-21 and Lev Rabbah 29:1. He notes that both underscore *God's grace*, and argues that unlike Rom 5:12-21, Adam is judged on the twelfth day (of his life in Eden) and granted a pardon on the first day of the seventh month (Rosh Hashanah, Lev 23:23–24).

41. A covenant (Heb. *berit*; Gk. *diathēkē*) is a solemn pact or agreement between two parties—e.g., a king with his vassals. Paul specifically mentions the covenants as a special possession of the Jewish people in Romans 9:4. One could easily argue that the "gifts and calling" in Romans 11:29, which Paul describes as "irrevocable," also include the covenants that God has made with Israel. See Puskas and Reasoner, *Letters of Paul*, 5–6.

42. Wright interprets "Israel" in Rom 11:26 as referring to a "spiritual Israel," a reconfigured people of God, i.e., the church, citing some church fathers for his support. *Climax,*, 250. Fitzmyer, nevertheless, shows that "all Israel" in the Hebrew Bible and later rabbinic writings refer to "historic, ethnic Israel" (623), in his *Roman*, 623–24. Wright's triumphalistic reading of Rom 11:26 also dissolves the mystery that Paul introduces to us in v. 25, which concerns the way or manner (currently hidden from us) in which Israel will ultimately be saved (cf. v. 33!). Today, we may well speculate about how a Jewish person might react to this idea of being included in God's family *via* Jesus Christ, but his or her reaction to the notion of *being excluded* from God's family (for whatever reason) requires no speculation about it's prompting a negative Jewish reaction! See Cook, *Jews Engage NT*, 163–75. See also an essay by Kaminisky and Reasoner that criticizes Wright's view, in my ch. II, nn23, 36.

"how much more will these natural branches [Israel?] be *grafted back into their own olive tree*," which is much easier to do with branches from *the same* tree (even if grafted in, later). Perhaps then the emphasis in Jenson's statement above (*ST* 2:363) is on "do not *need to be*" suggesting, perhaps, that the natural branch of historic Israel is "bent" down but not "broken off" (the above parentheses and *italics* are mine).[43]

Christian and Jewish Scholars on Romans 11

In his discussion of Romans 11:26 "all Israel will be saved," Christian scholar Arland Hultgren adds:

> "Has God rejected his people? By no means!" (Rom 11:1), "God has not rejected his people whom he foreknew (v. 2), "all Israel will be saved" (v. 26a; cf. *T. Benj.* 10.11; *m. Sanh.* 10.1), "as regards the gospel they are enemies . . . as regards election they are beloved" (v. 28), "for the gifts and calling of God are irrevocable" (Rom 11:29), and "God has imprisoned all in disobedience that he may be merciful to all" (v. 30; *NRSV*). It need not mean every individual, although "all Israel" denotes the people of Israel as a group, who have not received the gospel (11:28).[44]

Recent Jewish scholarship on Romans 11 is encouraging by offering plausible alternatives to older European interpretations that had written about the church as the "new" and "true" Israel because of the hardening

---

43. On "grafted into God's olive tree": Jewish scholar Mark Nanos makes the following supporting arguments: (a) the olive tree branches are "broken" or "bent" but *not* broken off (Rom 11:17-20) in his "'Broken Branches,'" 339-76; this argument addresses the problem of "re-grafting a natural branch" pointed out by Dunn, *Theology of Paul*, 525, n127, a book that Jenson cites as "the most convincing exegesis of Roman 9-11 known to me," *ST* 2:335, n74; Davies had earlier made this suggestion of "into and among, not instead of the branches lopped off," "Paul and the Gentiles," 155, 356. See http://www.marknanos.com/.

44. Hultgren, *Romans*, 419-20 (my summary of his discussion in the above paragraph). This exegesis from a Lutheran scholar is a refreshing alternative to "this judgment also falls upon their descendants, as can be seen with the Jews" (in the context of Rom 9-11), *Book of Concord*, 650. Historic Israel would include the faithful, hopeful, and helpless, all dependent on God's gracious action. In Galatians 3-4, Paul makes his case for *gentiles* to become children of promise without adhering to the Jewish observance of the law. See 1 Cor 9:20, where he does not condemn those Judeans who are "under the law." See also Paul's statements on the law and commandments as "holy, righteous, and good" (Rom 7:12), "faith working through love" (Gal 5:6; Rom 1:5), and love fulfilling the law (Rom 13:9-10).

of an obstinate and disobedient Israel "according to the flesh."[45] Mark Nanos, for example, has argued that "a protective callus has formed on Israel" until the full number of the gentiles comes in "then all Israel will be healed" (Rom 11:25).[46]

Although sensitive to issues raised in Romans 11, Jenson is keenly aware that the "sustained attention" of Jewish-Christian studies and the "need to use them with a certain bent" is "provoked by Europe's holocaust of the Jews." But this "new awareness should not principally be guilt but rather sober recognition of the history and its present mandate" that despite "the destruction of the city of Jerusalem in A.D. 70," Christian replacement theology, and the evil of "the Holocaust," the "urgent need for the church to appreciate in practice and theology" is "the fact that 'the Jewish way of life' did *not* in fact end" (*ST* 2:193).[47]

It should be mentioned here that Jenson includes in his *Theology*: Jewish dialogue partners who are not silent: Michael Wyschogrod[48] and David Novak (1:83, n63). Jenson even appeals to rabbinic sources in some of his arguments (1:76, n11; 1:83, n63). David Novak in turn agreed with Jenson's

---

45. Romans 9:8, alluding to Genesis 21:12c, also recalls the "righteous" remnant of Malachi 3:16-18, a *divine* action (Rom 11:5). According to Ezekiel 36:22-32, the remnant is a result of *God's* gracious action. Reflecting the older verdict of European scholarship, Craig Evans writes of Paul in Romans 11, "the Jews have left" the "company of the elect" in Evans, *To See and Not Perceive*, 85. Luther's 1543 treatise "Jews and their Lies" (*LW* 47:137-306) also alludes to Rom 10:2; 11:20, 28. In Hesse, *Das Verstockungsproblem*, a final sentence of doom is pronounced on a obstinate Israel, according to the author's frank interpretation of certain prophetic judgment speeches (e.g., Isa 9:13-21) and regarding most salvation oracles as later redactions.

46. Mark Nanos in his "'Callused,'" I also mentioned (my ch. II, n35) the sources he cited as evidence for his interpretation (e.g., Hippocrates, Galen, Celsus). See also updated article "Callused" with *pdf* on 5-6-10 in http://www.marknanos.com/. Dunn includes as an optional rendering of *pōrōsis* (Rom 11:25): "a callus which unites a fractured bone," *Romans 9-16*, 640.

47. I have not found the issue of Israeli Zionism discussed in Jenson's *Systematic Theology*, but it seems plausible to me that one can be a critic of current Israeli policies toward Palestinians without being anti-Jewish or anti-Semitic. See the efforts of Dr. Ned Hanauer, an American Jew, who is the executive director of *Search for Justice and Equality in Palestine/Israel*, Framingham, MA. See http://www.pdxjustice.org/node/39. See also Chomsky (a secular Jew), e.g., "Israel's West Bank Plans," *CNN.com*, August 16, 2013, and other recent articles in http://chomsky.info/articles.htm.

48. *ST* 1:43, n10, 59, 76-77, 85, 212; 2:123, n78. One of Wyschogrod's books that is cited favorably by Jenson several times is Wyschogrod, *The Body of Faith*. Wyschogrod has also written journal articles in *Pro Ecclesia*.

critique of "the West's Mediterranean pagan religious heritage . . . elevated to be the judge of its biblical heritage."[49]

Regarding the church's biblical heritage, Jenson writes "may Israel's holy book be so read, without violence to its coherence or historical actuality as to accept Jesus' resurrection and the appearance of the church as its own denouement" (1:30). Jenson seems to tread carefully here, perhaps aware of the issues raised, if one would assume that our Old Testament has little meaning without some reference to Jesus Christ. Are Jews today in a much less favorable position to comprehend the meaning of God's redemptive love in Scripture than are the Christians? Cannot both have an immediate and direct claim to our common biblical heritage as a "continuation of canonical Israel?" (*ST* 1:30, n23). Jenson adds that "the church has no prior reason *either* to defer to rabbinic exegesis *or* to read it as a priori false" (2:284).[50]

Concluding Thoughts

Although it may be a perplexing challenge in the church's preaching of the gospel and in theology's articulation of this effort, respectful consideration of the problem of Israel and the church is necessary to resume meaningful dialogue for the sake of a peaceful, mutual co-existence among all of God's people.[51]

49. Novak cites here Jenson *ST* 1:10 in his "Theology and Philosophy," 45. See also Rashkover and Kavka, *David Novak Reader*. Novak is also a contributor to Jenson's *Festschrift*, entitled *Trinity, Time & Church*, writing the article "Theology and Philosophy: An Exchange with Robert Jenson."

50. In Harrelson's review of "Bonhoeffer and the Bible" in *The Place of Bonhoeffer*, 115–42, Harrelson cautions against a "too rigorous" Christological interpretation of the OT. Dietrich Bonhoeffer, who opposed the *Reichskirche* and was executed by the Nazis in 1945, was occasionally prone to such a tendency (following the exegesis of Wilhelm Vischer), see ibid., 132 and 141, n31. Harrelson recommended (as a possible corrective) the more nuanced discussions of typology and Christological exegesis in Westermann, *Essays in OT*. "One reason for the distance Jewish biblicists tend to keep from biblical theology is the intense anti-Semitism evident in many of the classic works in the field." Levenson, *Hebrew Bible*, 40. Levenson cites Eichrodt, von Rad (to a lesser extent), and Wellhausen for denigrating Judaism in comparison with *Christianity as the new and true Israel*. The new biblical theology written by two German biblical scholars carefully avoids anti-Semitic supersessionism, see Feldmeier and Spieckermann, *God of the Living*, 9n16, 357, 396.

51. This study does not address the related and perhaps even more challenging issue of Islam's identity, along with that of Judaism and Christianity, as a member of Abraham's

APPENDIX: ON NATURAL AND GRAFTED BRANCHES

Is it an ancillary or necessary concern for an ecumenical theology to resume the new détente of the church with historic Israel, "Israel according to the flesh"? It is an important question if Israel had been hardened by God for the inclusion of the nations. I conclude with my own translation of the apostle Paul's words in Romans 11:

> But if some of the branches were bent down, and you a wild olive shoot, were grafted in among them to share in the nourishing root of the olive tree, boast not over the other branches, but if you boast [know] that it is not you that bears the root, but the root bears you. (Rom 11:17–18, AT).[52]

(and God's) family. Church statements like *Nostra Aetate* (of Vatican II), however, move in a commendable direction, by advocating tolerance and acceptance, and by emphasizing what is positive and edifying in all religions. See also Leonard Swidler et al., *Jews, Christians, and Muslims*; Mason, *Reading Abrahamic Faiths*.

52. The people of God grow out of the root of Israel. "For the apostle there is no salvation apart from the history of Israel" (Käsemann, *Romans*, 309–10). Mark Nanos observes: "This allegory is confronting any temptation of arrogance among the Christ-following non-Jewish audience toward the Israelites who are not Christ-proclaimers" (*JANT*, 277). The following admonition provides an appropriate ending here: "harden not your hearts" (Heb 3:15 citing Ps 95 [Ps 94 LXX]).

Bibliography

Abbreviations for journals (*JBL*, *NTS*), periodicals (*BA*), major reference works (*NIDB*), and series (LCL, NIGTC) follow those of *The SBL Handbook of Style: for Ancient Near Eastern, Biblical and Early Christian Studies*, 2nd ed., B. J. Collins, project Director, et al. Atlanta: SBL Press, 2014, and also *The Chicago Manual of Style*. 15th ed. Chicago: University of Chicago Press, 2003.

Abegg, Martin, Jr., Peter Flint, Eugene Ulrich. *The Dead Sea Scrolls Bible.* New York: HarperCollins, 1999.
Aeschylus. *Persians, Seven against Thebes, Suppliants, Prometheus Bound.* Allan. H. Sommerstein. LCL. Cambridge: Harvard University Press, 2008.
Aland, Kurt, ed. *Synopsis Quattuor Evangeliorum.* 12th ed. Stuttgart: German Bible Society, 1983.
Aland, Kurt, Matthew Black, et al. eds. *The Greek New Testament.* 4th rev. ed. Barbara Aland et al. Stuttgart: Bibelgesellschaft, 1998.
Albl, Martin C. *And Scripture Cannot Be Broken: The Form and Function of the Early Christian Testimonia Collections.* NovTSup. Leiden: Brill, 1999.
Alcoholics Anonymous. 4th ed. New York: A. A. World Services, 2001.
Analytical Lexicon to the Septuagint. Exp. ed., Bernard A. Taylor et. al. Peabody, MA: Hendrickson, 2009.
Anderson, Paul N. "Bakhtin's Dialogism and the Corrective Rhetoric of the Johannine Misunderstanding Dialogue: Exposing Seven Crises in the Johannine Situation." In *Bakhtin and Genre in Biblical Studies*, edited by Roland Boer, 133–59. Semeia 63. Atlanta: SBL, 2007.
———. "John and Qumran: Discovery and Interpretation over Sixty Years." In *John, Qumran, and the Dead Sea Scrolls: Sixty Years of Discovery and Debate*, edited by Mary Coloe et al., 15–50. Early Judaism and its Literature 32. Atlanta: SBL, 2011.

BIBLIOGRAPHY

Anderson, R. Dean, Jr., *Glossary of Greek Rhetorical Terms Connected to Methods of Argumentation, Figures and Tropes from the Anximenes to Quintillian.* CBET 24. Leuven: Peters, 2000.

The Ante-Nicene Fathers. Edited by Alexander Roberts and James Donaldson. 1885–87. 10 vols. Reprint, Peabody, MA: Hendrickson, 1994. Abbreviation: *ANF.*

Archer, Gleason L., and Gregory Chirichigno. *Old Testament Quotations in the New Testament.* 1983. Reprint, Eugene, OR: Wipf and Stock, 2005.

Arnold, B. T. "Pentateuchal Criticism, History of." In *The Dictionary of the Pentateuch*, edited by T. D. Alexander and D. W. Baker, 622–31. Downers Grove, IL: IVP, 2003.

Assmann, Jan. "Zur Geschichte des Herzens im Alten Ägypten." In *Die Erfindung des inneren Menschen: Studien zur religiösen Anthropologie*, edited by Jan Assmann, 81–113. SVfR 6. Gütersloh: Gütersloher Verl.-Haus Mohn, 1993.

Attridge, Harold W. *The Epistle to the Hebrews.* Hermeneia. Minneapolis: Fortress, 1989.

Augustine. *Confessions.* Translated by R. Pines-Coffin. New York: Penguin, 2003.

———. *Homilies on the First Epistle of John.* Vol. III/14. The Works of Saint Augustine: A Translation for the 21st Century. Translated by Boniface Ramsay. Hyde Park, NY: New City Press, 2008.

Aune, David E. *The New Testament in Its Literary Environment.* LEC. Edited by Wayne Meeks. Philadelphia: Westminster, 1987.

———. *Revelation 1–5.* WBC 52A. Dallas: Word, 1997.

———. *Revelation 6–16.* WBC 52B. Dallas: Word, 1998.

———. *Revelation 17–22.* WBC 52C. Dallas: Word, 1998.

———. *The Westminster Dictionary of New Testament and Early Christian Literature and Rhetoric.* Louisville, KY: Westminster John Knox, 2003.

Austin, J. L. *How to Do Things with Words: The William James Lectures.* 2nd ed. J. O. Urmson. Cambridge: Harvard University Press, 1975.

Bailey, James L., and Lyle D. Vander Broek. *Literary Forms in the New Testament: A Handbook.* Louisville, KY: Westminster John Knox, 1992.

Baker, Kimberly. *Augustine's Doctrine of the Totus Christus: Reflecting on the Church as Sacrament of Unity.* Cambridge: Cambridge University Press, 2013.

Bakhtin, Mikhail M. *The Dialogic Imagination: Four Essays.* University of Texas Slavid Series. Translated by Michael Holmquist and Caryl Emerson. Austin: University of Texas, 1981.

Baltzer, Klaus. *Deutero-Isaiah: A Commentary on Isaiah 40–55.* Hermeneia; Fortress, 2001.

Barr, James. *Biblical Words for Time.* London: SCM, 1962.

———. "Common Sense and Biblical Language" *Biblica* 49 (1968) 377–87.

———. *Semantics of Biblical Language.* London: Oxford, 1961.

Barrett, C. K. *The Gospel According to John.* 2nd ed. London: SPCK, 1978.

———. *The New Testament Background: Selected Documents.* SPCK, 1956. Rev. and exp. ed. New York: HarperCollins, 1989.

Barth, Karl. *Church Dogmatics: The Doctrine of Creation, Part 2.* Vol. III. Translated by G. W. Bromiley, and T. F. Torrance. London: T. & T.Clark, 2004.

Basinger, David, and Randall Basinger, eds. *Predestination and Free Will: Four Views of Divine Sovereignty & Human Freedom.* Downers Grove, IL: IVP, 1986.

Bauckham, Richard, and Carl Mosser, eds. *The Gospel of John and Christian Theology.* Grand Rapids: Eerdmans, 2008.

Bauer, Walter, Frederick William Danker, W. F. Arndt, and F. W. Gingrich, eds. *A Greek-English Lexicon of the New Testament and Other Early Christian Literature.* Revised by W. F. Danker. 3rd ed. Chicago: University of Chicago Press, 2000. Abbreviation: BDAG.

Beale, G. K., and D. A. Carson, eds. *Commentary on the New Testament Use of the Old Testament*. Grand Rapids: Baker Academic, 2007.

———. "An Exegetical and Theological Consideration of the Hardening of Pharaoh's Heart in Exodus 4–14 and Romans 9." *TJ* 5 (1984) 129–54.

Beasley-Murray, George R. *John*. WBC 36. 2nd ed. Dallas: Word, 1999.

Bechtel, L. M. "Genesis 2.4b—3.24: A Myth about Human Maturation." *JSOT* 67 (1995) 3–26.

BeDuhn, Jason D. *The First Testament: Marcion's Scriptural Canon*. Salem, OR: Polebridge, 2013.

Ben-Johanan, Karma. *Jacob's Younger Brother: Christian-Jewish Relations after Vatican II*. Cambridge: Belknap, 2022.

Betz, Hans Dieter. *Galatians: A Commentary on Paul's Letter to the Churches in Galatia*. Hermeneia. Minneapolis: Fortress, 1989.

———. *The Greek Magical Papyri in Translation, including the Demotic Spells*. 2nd ed. Chicago: University of Chicago Press, 1996.

Biblia Hebraica Stuttgartensia. Rev. ed. Edited by H. Van Dyke Parunak, Richard Whitaker, Emanuel Tov, Alan Groves et al. Stuttgart: Deutsche Bibelgesellschaft, 1990.

Bieringer, Didier Pollefeyt, F. Vandcasteele-Vanneuville, eds. *Anti-Judaism and the Fourth Gospel*. Louisville, KY: Westminster John Knox, 2001.

Black. Matthew. *An Aramaic Approach to the Gospels and Acts*. 1946. 3rd ed. Reprint. Peabody, MA: Hendrickson, 1998.

Blackman, Philip. *Mishnayoth: Pointed Hebrew Text, English Translation, Introductions, Notes, Supplement*. 7 Vols. New York: Judaica Press, 1964.

Blass, Friedrich W., and Albert Debrunner. *A Greek Grammar of the New Testament and Other Early Christian Literature*. Translated and revised by Robert. W. Funk with supplementary notes of A. Debrunner. Chicago: University of Chicago Press, 1961.

Blenkinsopp, Joseph. *The Pentateuch*. New York: Doubleday, 1992.

Block, Daniel I. *The Book of Ezekiel 1–24*. NICOT. Grand Rapids: Eerdmans, 1997.

———. *Book of Ezekiel 25–48*. NICOT. Grand Rapids: Eerdmans, 1998.

Bokser, Baruch K. "Unleavened Bread and Passover, Feasts of." In *AYBD* 6:755–65.

The Book of Concord. Edited by Robert Kolb and Timothy J. Wengert et al. Minneapolis: Fortress, 2000.

Botterweck, G. Johannes, Helmer Ringgren, and Heinz-Josef Fabry, eds. *Theological Dictionary of the Old Testament*. Translated by John T. Willis et al. 17 vols. Grand Rapids: Eerdmans, 1977–2018. Abbreviation: *TDOT*.

Boyarin, Daniel. *Intertextuality and the Reading of the Midrash*. 1990. Reprint, Eugene, OR: Wipf and Stock, 2001.

Boustan, Ra'anan. "Hekhalot Literature." In *EDEJ* 710–21.

Braaten, Carl E., and Robert W. Jenson, eds. *Jews and Christians: People of God*. Grand Rapids: Eerdmans, 2003.

———. "Eschatology and Mission in the Theology of Robert Jenson." In *Trinity, Time and Church: A Response to the Theology of Robert W. Jenson*, edited by Colin Gunston, 298–311. Grand Rapids: Eerdmans, 2000.

Brant, Jo-Ann. *Dialogue and Drama: Elements of Greek Tragedy in the Fourth Gospel*. Peabody, MA: Hendrickson, 2004.

Brooke, George J. *The Dead Sea Scrolls and the New Testament*. Minneapolis: Fortress, 2005.
Brown, Alexandra R. *The Cross and Human Transformation: Paul's Apocalyptic Word in 1 Corinthians*. Minneapolis: Fortress, 1995.
Brown, Francis, Samuel R. Driver, and Charles A. Briggs. *Brown-Driver-Briggs Hebrew and English Lexicon*. Reprint, Oxford: Clarendon, 1977. Abbreviation: BDB.
Brown, Raymond E. *The Epistles of John. A New Translation with Introduction and Commentary* AYB 30. New Haven, CT: Yale University Press, 1982.
———. *The Gospel According to John XIII–XXI. A New Translation with Introduction and Commentary*. AYB 29. New Haven, CT: Yale University Press, 1966.
———. *The Gospel According to John I–XII. A New Translation with Introduction and Commentary*. AYB 29. New Haven, CT: Yale University Press, 1970.
Brueggemann, Walter. *1 & 2 Kings*. Macon, GA: Smyth & Helwys, 2000.
———. *Reverberations of Faith: A Theological Handbook of Old Testament Themes*. Louisville, KY: Westminster John Knox, 2002.
———. *Theology of the Old Testament: Testimony, Dispute, Advocacy*. Minneapolis: Fortress, 2012.
Bultmann, Rudolf. *Die Geschichte der synoptischen Tradition*, 1921. *The History of the Synoptic Tradition*. Translated by John Marsh. 1963. Rev. ed. 1976. Reprint, Peabody, MA: Hendrickson, 1994.
———. *The Gospel of John: A Commentary*. Translated by G. Beasley-Murray et al. 1971. Reprint, Eugene, OR: Wipf & Stock, 2014
———. *Theology of the New Testament: Complete in One Volume*. Translated by K. Grobel. New York: Scribner's Sons, 1955.
Burkert, Walter. *Ancient Mystery Cults*. Cambridge: Harvard University Press, 1987.
———. *Greek Religion*. Translated by John Raffan. Cambridge: Harvard University Press, 1985.
Burridge, Richard A. *Imitating Jesus: An Inclusive Approach to New Testament Ethics*. Grand Rapids: Eerdmans, 2007.
———. *What Are the Gospels? A Comparison with Graeco-Roman Biography*. A Twenty-fifth Anniversary Edition. Waco, TX: Baylor University Press, 2018.
Calvin, John. *Institutes of the Christian Religion*. 1581 ed. Translated by Henry Beveridge, 1845. Bellingham, WA: Logos Bible Software, 1997.
Cameron, J. M. "The Bible and Legal Medicine." *Medicine, Science and Law*, January, 1970, 7–13.
Caragounis, Chrys C. *The Development of Greek and the New Testament: Morphology, Syntax, Phonology, and Textual Transmission*. WUNT 167. Tübingen: Mohr Siebeck, 2004.
Carroll, Robert P. "Blindsight and the Vision Thing: Blindness and Insight in the Book of Isaiah." In *Writing and Reading the Scroll of Isaiah*, edited by Craig C. Broyles and Craig A. Evans, 79–93. VT 70.1. Leiden: Brill, 1997.
Cartlidge, David R., and David L. Dungan, eds. *Documents for the Study of the Gospels*. Rev. ed. Minneapolis: Fortress, 1994.
Casssell's Latin Dictionary. Edited by D. P. Simpson. New York: Macmillan, 1968.
Cassidy, Richard, ed. *Society and Politics in the Acts of the Apostles*. Maryknoll, NY: Orbis, 1987.
Cassuto, Umberto. *A Commentary on the Book of Exodus*. Translated by Israel Abrahams. Jerusalem: Magnes, 1974.

Charles, R. H. *Commentary on the Apocrypha of the Old Testament*. Oxford: Clarendon, 1913.
Charlesworth, James H., ed. *The Dead Sea Scrolls: Hebrew, Aramaic, and Greek Texts with English Translations*. Tübingen: Mohr Siebeck, 1994.
———. *Jesus as Mirrored in John: The Genius in the New Testament*. London: Bloomsbury Academic, 2019.
———, ed. *The Messiah: Developments in Earliest Judaism and Christianity*. First Princeton Symposium on Judaism and Christian Origins. Minneapolis: Fortress, 1992.
———, ed. *The Odes of Solomon*. Pseudepigrapha Series, 7. Missoula, MT: Scholars, 1978.
———, ed. *The Old Testament Pseudepigrapha*. 2 vols. Garden City, NY: Doubleday, 1983, 1985.
Childs, Brevard S. *The Book of Exodus: A Critical, Theological Commentary*. OTL. Philadelphia: Westminster, 1974.
Chilton, Bruce, and Craig A. Evans. *Studying the Historical Jesus: Evaluations of the State of Current Research*. NTTS 19. Leiden: Brill 1994.
Chomsky Noam "Israel's West Bank Plans Will Leave Palestinians Very Little." CNN.com, August 16, 2013. http://chomsky.info/articles.htm
Christensen, Duane L. "The Nations." In *AYBD* 4:1037–49.
Cicero. *De Senectute, De Amicitia, De Divinatione*. Translated by William A. Falconer, LCL. Cambridge: Harvard University Press, 1922.
Celsus, Aulus Cornelius. *De Medicina*. Translated by W. G. Spencer. LCL. Cambridge: Harvard University Press, 1935.
Ceresko, Anthony R. "The Identity of 'the Blind' and 'the Lame' in 2 Sam 5:8b." *CBQ* 63 (2001) 23–30.
Clayton, Philip, James W. Walters, and John Martin Fischer. *What's with Free Will? Ethics and Religion after Neuroscience*. Eugene, OR: Cascade Books, 2020.
Clement of Alexandria. *Exhortation to the Greeks, The Rich Man's Salvation, and To the Newly Baptized*. Translated by G. W. Butterworth. LCL. Cambridge: Harvard University Press, 1953.
Clère, J. J. "L'expression dné mhwt des autobiographies égyptiennes." *JEA* 35 (1949) 38–41
Coats, George W. *Exodus 1–18*. FOTL. Grand Rapids: Eerdmans, 1999.
Coggins, R. J., and J. L. Houlden, eds. *Dictionary of Biblical Interpretation*. London: SCM, 1990.
Cohen, Shaye J. D. *From the Maccabees to the Mishnah*. Library of Early Christianity. Vol 7. Louisville, KY: Westminster John Knox, 1988.
———. "Ioudaios." In *EDEJ* 769–70.
———. "The Significance of Yavneh: Pharisees, Rabbis, and the End of Jewish Sectarianism." *Hebrew Union College Annual* 55 (1984) 27–53.
Collins, John J., Craig A. Evans, and Lee Martin McDonald. *Ancient Jewish and Christian Scriptures: New Developments in Canon Controversy*. Louisville, KY: Westminster John Knox, 2020.
Collins, John J. *Beyond the Qumran Community: The Sectarian Movement of the Dead Sea Scrolls*. Grand Rapids: Eerdmans, 2010.
———. "Canon, Canonization." In *EDEJ* 460–63.
———. *Jewish Cult and Hellenistic Culture: Essays on the Jewish Encounter with Hellenism and Roman Rule*. Leiden: Brill, 2005.
Collins, John J., and Daniel C. Harlow, eds. *Dictionary of Early Judaism*. Grand Rapids: Eerdmans, 2010. Abbreviation: *EDEJ*.

BIBLIOGRAPHY

Comfort, Philip. *Encountering the Manuscripts: An Introduction to New Testament Paleography and Textual Criticism.* Nashville: Broadman & Holman, 2005.

Comfort, Philip, and David P. Barrett, eds. *The Complete Text of the Earliest New Testament Manuscripts.* Grand Rapids: Baker, 1999.

Conrad, Edgar W. "Remnant." *NIDB* 4:761–62.

Cook, Michael. *Modern Jews Engage the New Testament: Enhancing Jewish Well-Being in a Christian Environment.* Woodstock, VT: Jewish Lights, 2012.

Cox, Dorian G. Coover. "The Hardening of Pharaoh's Heart in Its Literary and Cultural Contexts, *BSac* 163 (July-Sept 2006) 202–311.

Cox, Roger L. "Tragedy and the Gospel Narratives." In *The Bible in Its Literary Milieu*, edited by Vincent L. Tollers et al., 298–317. Grand Rapids: Eerdmans, 1979.

Craigie, Peter C. *The Book of Deuteronomy.* NICOT. Grand Rapids: Eerdmans, 1976.

Cryer, Frederick H., and Thomas L. Thompson, eds., *Qumran between the Old and New Testaments.* JSOT Supplement Series, 290. Sheffield, UK: Sheffield Academic Press, 1998.

Culpepper, R. Alan. *The Anatomy of the Fourth Gospel: A Study in Literary Design.* Philadelphia: Fortress, 1983.

———. *The Johannine School: An Examination of the Johannine-School Hypothesis Based on the Investigation of the Nature of Ancient Schools.* SBLDS 26. Missoula, MT: Scholars, 1975.

Cullmann, Oscar. *Salvation in History.* NTL. New York: Harper & Row, 1967.

Cunningham, Philip A. "The Triune One, The Incarnate Logos, and Israel's Covenantal Life." In *Christ Jesus and the Jewish People Today: New Explorations of Theological Interrelationships*, edited by Philip Cunningham et al., 183–201. Grand Rapids: Eerdmans, 2011.

Cunningham, Philip A., and Joseph Sievers, et al., eds. *Christ Jesus and the Jewish People Today: New Explorations of Theological Interrelationships.* Grand Rapids: Eerdmans, 2011.

Currid, John D. *Ancient Egypt and the Old Testament.* Grand Rapids: Baker, 1997.

———. "Why Did God Harden Pharaoh's Heart?" *BRev*, December 1998, 47–51

Danby, Herbert. *The Mishnah: Translated from the Hebrew with Introduction and Brief Explanatory Notes.* Oxford: Oxford University Press, 1933.

Daniélou, Jean. *The Theology of Jewish Christianity.* Vol. 1. *History of Early Christian Doctrine before the Council of Nicea.* Translated and edited by John Baker. Philadelphia: Westminster, 1977.

Danker, Frederick W. "Hardness of Heart: A Study in Biblical Thematic." *CTM* 44.2 (1972) 89–100.

Dann, Moshe. "Why Pharaoh's Heart Hardened." *Jerusalem Post* 22.03. January 2, 2014. jpost.com.

Daube, David. *Ancient Jewish Law: Three Inaugural Lectures.* Leiden: Brill, 1988.

———. *The New Testament and Rabbinic Judaism.* Jordan Lectures. 1956. Reprint, Eugene, OR: Wipf and Stock, 2011.

Davies, W. D. *Introduction to the Pharisees.* Philadelphia: Fortress, 1967.

———. *Paul and Rabbinic Judaism.* 4th ed. Philadelphia: Fortress, 1980.

———. "Paul and the Gentiles: A Suggestion Concerning Romans 11:13–24." In *Jewish and Pauline Studies*, 153–63. Philadelphia: Fortress, 1984.

Davies, W. D., and Dale C. Allison, Jr. *A Critical and Exegetical Commentary on the Gospel According to Saint Matthew.* ICC. 2 Vols. London: T. & T. Clark, 2004.

deClaissé-Walford, Nancy, Beth L. Tanner, Rolf A. Jacobson. *The Book of Psalms*. NICOT. Grand Rapids: Eerdmans, 2014.

Deissmann, Adolf. *Light from the Ancient East: The New Testament Illustrated by Recently Discovered Texts of the Graeco-Romans World*. Translated by Lionel R. M. Strachan from 1932 ed. of *Licht vom Osten*. Grand Rapids: Baker, 1978.

Deleuze, Gilles. "Plato and the Simulacrum." Translated by M. Lester and C. Stivale. In *The Logic of Sense*, 253–66. New York: Columbia University Press, 1990.

Demosthenes. *Against Meidias, Against Androtion, Against Aristocrates, Against Timocrates, Against Aristogeiton 1 and 2*. Translated by J. H. Vince. LCL. Cambridge: Harvard University Press, 1935.

Dines, Jennifer. *The Septuagint*. UBW. New York: Continuum, 2004

Di Tomasso, Lorenzo. *A Bibliography of Pseudepigrapha Research 1850–1999*. JSPSup 39. Sheffield, UK: Sheffield Academic Press, 2001.

The Documents of Vatican II. Edited by Walter M. Abbott, S. J. et al. America Press, 1963–65. https://www.vatican.va/archive/histcouncils/iivaticancouncil/index.htm

Dodd, C. H. *According to the Scriptures: The Sub-Structure of New Testament Theology*. London: Nesbit, 1952.

———. *The Interpretation of the Fourth Gospel*. London: Cambridge University Press, 1968.

Dodds, E. R. *Euripides Bacchae*. 2nd ed. Oxford: Clarendon, 1960.

———. *The Greeks and the Irrational*. Berkeley: University of California Press, 1951.

———. *Pagan and Christian in an Age of Anxiety*. London: Cambridge University Press, 1965.

Donin, Hayim Halevy. *To Be A Jew: A Guide to Jewish Observance in Contemporary Life*. New York: Basic, 1972.

Dozeman, Thomas B. *Commentary on Exodus*. ECC. Grand Rapids: Eerdmans, 2009.

Driver, Samuel R. *The Book of Exodus*, CBSC. Cambridge: Cambridge University Press, 1918.

———. *An Introduction to the Literature of the Old Testament*. New York: Scribner's Sons, 1914.

Drower, E. S. *The Canonical Prayerbook of the Mandeans*. Leiden: Brill, 1957.

Dunn, James D. G. *Beginnings from Jerusalem: Christianity in the Making*. Vol. 2. Grand Rapids: Eerdmans, 2009.

———. *Christology in the Making: An Inquiry into the Origins of the Doctrine of Incarnation*. 2nd ed. London: SCM, 1989.

———. *Jews and Christians: The Parting of the Ways, AD 70 to 135*. 1992. Reprint, Grand Rapids: Eerdmans, 1999.

———. *Romans 9–16*. WBC 38B. Waco, TX: Word, 1988.

Ehrman, Bart D. *The Orthodox Corruption of Scripture: The Effect of Early Christological Controversies on the Text of the New Testament*. New York: Oxford University Press, 1993.

Ehrman, Bart D., and Michael W. Holmes. *The Text of the New Testament in Contemporary Research: Essays on the Status Quaestionis*. SD no. 46. Grand Rapids: Eerdmans, 1995.

Eichrodt, Walther. *Theology of the Old Testament*. Translated by J. A. Baker. 2 vols. Louisville, KY: Westminster John Knox, 1961–67.

Eising, Hermann. "Die ägyptischen Plagen." In *Lex tua ventas—Festschrift fur Hubert Junker*, edited by H. Gross and F. Mussner, 75–87. Trier: Pauhnus Verlag, 1961.

Elliott, John H. "A Catholic Gospel: Reflections on 'Early Catholicism' in the NT." *CBQ* 31 (1969) 213–23.
———. "Jesus the Israelite Was Neither a Jew nor a Christian: On Correcting Misleading Nomenclature." *JSHJ* 5 (2007)119–54.
———. *What Is Social-Science Criticism?* GBS NT. Minneapolis: Fortress, 1993.
Ellis, E. Earle. *The Old Testament in Early Christianity: Canon and Interpretation in the Light of Modern Research.* Tübingen: Mohr Siebeck, 1991. Grand Rapids: Baker, 1992.
Elwell, Walter A., and Robert W. Yarbrough. *Readings from the First-Century World.* EBS. Grand Rapids: Baker, 1998.
Enns, Peter. *Exodus.* NIV Application Commentary. Grand Rapids: Zondervan, 2000.
Ericksen, Robert P. *Theologians under Hitler: Gerhard Kittel, Paul Althaus and Emmanuel Hirsch.* New Haven, CT: Yale University Press, 1985.
Erman, Adolf, and Herman Grapow, et al. *Wörterbuch der aegyptischen Sprache.* 7 vols. Leipzig: Hinrichs, 1926–63.
Esler, Philip F. *Modeling Early Christianity: Social Scientific Studies of the NT in Its Context.* London: Routledge, 1995.
Euripides: Bacchanals, Madness of Hercules. Translated by Arthur S. Way. Vol. 3. LCL. Cambridge: Harvard University Press, 1988.
Evans, Craig A., ed. *Ancient Texts for New Testament Studies: A Guide to Background Literature.* Peabody, MA: Hendrickson, 2005.
———. "Introduction: An Aramaic Approach Thirty Years Later." Introduction to Matthew Black's *An Aramaic Approach to the Gospels and Acts.* 3rd ed. Reprint, Peabody, MA: Hendrickson, 1998.
———. *To See and Not Perceive: Isaiah 6.9–10 in Early Jewish and Christian Interpretation.* JSOTSup. 64. Sheffield, UK: Sheffield Academic Press, 1989.
Evans, Craig A., and James A. Sanders. *Early Christian Interpretation of the Scriptures of Israel: Investigations and Proposals.* Sheffield, UK: Sheffield Academic Press, 1997.
Evans, Craig A., Robert L. Webb, and Richard A. Wiebe, eds., *Nag Hammadi Texts and the Bible: A Synopsis and Index.* NT Tools and Studies, 18. Leiden: Brill, 1993.
Exodus Rabbah. See https://www.sefaria.org/ShemotRabbah
Fabry, Heinz-Josef, "לֵב." In *TDOT* 7:399–437.
Farmer, William R. *Maccabees, Zealots and Josephus.* New York: Columbia University Press, 1956.
Feinberg, John S. "God Ordains All Things." In *Predestination and Free Will: Four Views of Divine Sovereignty & Human Freedom,* edited by David Basinger and Randall Basinger, 17–44. Downers Grove, IL: IVP, 1986.
Feldmeier, Reinhard, and Hermann Spieckermann. *God of the Living: A Biblical Theology.* Translated by M. E. Biddle. Waco, TX: Baylor, 2011.
Fensham, F. Charles. *The Books of Ezra and Nehemiah.* NICOT. Grand Rapids: Eerdmans, 1982.
Ferguson, Everett. *Backgrounds of Early Christianity.* 3rd ed. Grand Rapids: Eerdmans, 2003.
Finegan, Jack. *Handbook of Biblical Chronology: Principles of Time Reckoning in the Ancient World and Problems of Chronology in the Bible.* 2nd ed. rev. & exp. Peabody, MA: Hendrickson, 1998.
———. *Myth and Mystery. An Introduction to the Pagan Religions of the Biblical World.* Baker, 1989.

Finkelstein, Louis. *The Pharisees: The Sociological Background of Their Faith.* 2 vols. 3rd ed. Philadelphia: Jewish Publication Society, 1963.

Fishbane, Michael. "Use, Authority and Interpretation of Mikra at Qumran." In *Mikra: Text, Translation, Reading and Interpretation of the Hebrew Bible in Ancient Judaism and Early Christianity*, edited by M. J. Mulder, 339–77. Assen, NL: van Gorcum, 1988.

Fitzmyer, Joseph A. *A Guide to the Dead Sea Scrolls and Related Literature.* Rev. and exp. ed. Grand Rapids: Eerdmans, 2008.

———. "The Languages of Palestine in the First Century." *CBQ* 32.4 (1970) 501–31

———. *Romans: A New Translation with Introduction and Commentary.* YAB. New Haven, CT: Yale, 1992.

———. *The Semitic Background of the New Testament.* Biblical Resources Series. A Combined edition of *Essays on The Semitic Background of the New Testament* and *A Wandering Aramean: Collected Aramaic Essays.* Grand Rapids: Eerdmans, 1997.

Flusser, David. *Judaism of the Second Temple Period, Volume 2: The Jewish Sages and Their Literature.* Grand Rapids: Eerdmans, 2009.

———. *Judaism of the Second Temple Period, Volume 1: Qumran and Apocalypticism.* Translated by Azzan Yadin. Grand Rapids: Eerdmans, 2007.

Flusser, David, and R. Steven Notley. *The Sage from Galilee: Rediscovering Jesus' Genius.* Grand Rapids: Eerdmans, 2007.

Ford, William A. *God, Pharaoh and Moses: Explaining the Lord's Actions in the Exodus Plagues Narrative.* PBM. Eugene, OR: Wipf and Stock, 2007.

Foerster, Werner. *Gnosis: A Selection of Gnostic Texts.* 2 vols. Translated by R. McL. Wilson. Oxford: Clarendon, 1972–74.

Fowler, Robert M. "The Rhetoric of Direction and Indirection in the Gospel of Mark." *Semeia* 48 (1989) 115–34.

Fragments: The Collected Wisdom of Heraclitus. Translated by Brook Haxton, with foreword by James Hillman. New York: Viking, 2001.

Freedman, David Noel, ed. *The Anchor Yale Bible Dictionary.* 6 vols. New Haven, CT: Yale University Press, 1992.

Fretheim, Terence E. *Deuteronomic History.* Nashville: Abingdon, 1983.

———. *Exodus.* Interpretation. Louisville, KY: Westminster John Knox, 1991.

———. *The Pentateuch.* Nashville: Abingdon, 1996.

Frey, Jörg, Jens Herzer, et al. *Pseudepigraphie und Verfasssserfiktion in frühchristlichen Briefen. Pseudepigraphy and Author Fiction in Early Christian Letters.* Tübingen: Mohr Siebeck, 2009.

Fritz, Volkmar. *1 & 2 Kings.* CC. Translated by A. Hagedorn. Minneapolis: Fortress, 2003.

Funk, Robert W. and the Jesus Seminar. *The Five Gospels: The Search for the Authentic Words of Jesus.* New York: Polebridge and Macmillan, 1993.

Furnish, Victor Paul. *II Corinthians: Translated with Introduction, Notes, and Commentary.* Vol. 32A. AYB. New Haven, CT: Yale University Press, 2008.

Gadamer, Hans-Georg. *Truth and Method.* 2nd rev. ed. Translated by Joel Weinsheimer and Donald G. Marshall. New York: Continuum, 1994.

Galen, *The Art of Medicine.* Translated by Ian Johnston. LCL. Cambridge: Harvard University Press, 2016.

Gamble, Harry Y. "Amanuensis." In *AYBD* 1:172–73.

———. *Books and Readers in the Early Church: A History of Early Christian Texts.* New Haven, CT: Yale University Press, 1995.

———. *The New Testament Canon: Its Making and Meaning.* 1985. Reprint, Eugene, OR: Wipf & Stock, 2002.
Garcia Martinez, Florentino. *The Dead Sea Scrolls Translated. The Qumran Texts in English.* 1994. Grand Rapids: Eerdmans, 1996.
———, ed. *Wisdom and Apocalypticism in the Dead Sea Scrolls and in the Biblical Tradition.* BETL 168; Leuven: Peeters, 2003.
Garcia Martinez, Florentino, and Eibert J. C. Tigchelaar, eds. *The Dead Sea Scrolls: Study Edition.* 2nd ed. 2 vols. 1997. US ed. Grand Rapids: Eerdmans, 1999.
Garland, David E. *2 Corinthians.* NAC. Nashville: Broadman & Holman, 1999.
Garrett, Duane A. *A Commentary on Exodus.* Grand Rapids: Kregel, 2014.
Garroway, Joshua D. "*Ioudiaos.*" In *JANT*, 524–25.
Gaventa, Beverly Roberts, and Richard B. Hays, eds. *Seeking the Identity of Jesus: A Pilgrimage.* Grand Rapids: Eerdmans, 2008.
Gerhardsson, Birger. *Memory and Manuscript: Oral Tradition and Written Transmission in Rabbinic Judaism and Early Christianity with Tradition and Transmission in Early Christianity.* Translated by Eric Sharpe. 2nd ed. BRS. Grand Rapids: Eerdmans, 1998.
Gerstenberger, Erhard S. *Psalms, Part 2 and Lamentations.* FOTL. Grand Rapids: Eerdmans, 2001.
Gesenius' Hebrew Grammar. 2nd ed. Edited by H. F. W. Gesenius, E. Kautzsch, A. E. Cowley. Oxford: Clarendon, 1910. Abbreviation: GKC.
Gillingham, Susan. *Psalms through the Centuries: A Reception Commentary on Psalms 1–72.* Wiley Blackwell Bible Commentaries, 2. Hoboken, NJ: Wiley-Blackwell, 2018.
Gnilka, Joachim. *Die Verstockung Israels. Isaias 6:9–10 in the Theology of Synoptics.* STANT 3. Munich: Kosel-Verlag, 1961.
Goldin, Judah. *The Fathers According to Rabbi Nathan.* Yale Judaica Series. New Haven, CT: Yale University Press, 1955.
Goldingay, John. *The Book of Jeremiah.* NICOT. Grand Rapids: Eerdmans, 2021.
———. *Do We Need the New Testament? Letting the Old Testament Speak for Itself.* Downers Grove, IL: IVP Academic, 2015.
———. *Theological Diversity and the Authority of the Old Testament.* Grand Rapids: Eerdmans, 1987.
Green, David, and Richard Lattimore, eds. *The Complete Greek Tragedies Euripides V: Electra, The Phoenician Women, The Bacchae.* With a Chronological Note by Richard Lattimore. Chicago: University Press of Chicago, 1959.
Green, Joel B., and Scot McKnight, eds. *Dictionary of Jesus and the Gospels.* Downers Grove, IL: IVP, 2002.
———, ed. *Hearing the New Testament: Strategies for Interpretation.* 2nd ed. Grand Rapids: Eerdmans, 2010.
Grenfell, Bernard P., and Arthur S. Hunt, eds. *New Classical Fragments and Other Greek and Latin Papyri.* London: Oxford University Press, 1897.
Gritsch, Eric W. *Martin Luther's Anti-Semitism: Against His Better Judgment.* Grand Rapids: Eerdmans, 2012.
Grumach, Irene. *Untersuchungen zur Lebenslehre des Amено.* Munich: Deutscher Kunstverlag, 1972.
Guggenheimer, Heinrich W., ed. *The Jerusalem Talmud. First Order: Zeraim Tractate Berakhot.* Studia Judaica, Bd. 18. Berlin: de Gruyter, 2000.

Guide to Resources in Rabbinic Literature. State University of New York at Albany. See online http://library.albany.edu/subject/guides/GuidetoResourcesinRabbinicLiterature.html.
Guirard, Felix, ed. *New Larousse Encyclopedia of Mythology*. New ed. Translated by D. Ames and R. Aldington. London: Hamlyn, 1968.
Gunton, Colin, ed. *Trinity, Time and Church: A Response to the Theology of Robert W. Jenson*. Grand Rapids: Eerdmans, 2000.
Gupta, Nijay K. "Faith." In *The Lexham Bible Dictionary*, edited by John D. Barry et al. Bellingham, WA: Lexham, 2016.
Guthrie, W. K. C. *The Greeks and their Gods*. Boston: Beacon, 1951.
Hahneman, G. M. T. *Muratorian Fragment and the Development of the Canon*. Oxford: Oxford University Press, 1992.
———. "The Muratorian Fragment and the Origins of the New Testament Canon." In *The Canon Debate*, edited by Lee Martin McDonald, James A. Sanders, 405–15. Peabody, MA: Hendrickson, 2002.
Hanauer, Ned. *Search for Justice and Equality in Palestine/Israel*. Framingham, MA. http://www.pdxjustice.org/node/39.
Harmon, Matthew S. *Rebels and Exiles: A Biblical Theology of Sin and Restoration*. Downers Grove, IL: IVP Academic, 2020.
Harnack, Adolf von. *Marcion: The Gospel of an Alien God*. Translated by J. E. Steely and L. D. Bierma; Grand Rapids: Baker, 1990.
Harris, J. Rendel, and Alphonse Mingana, eds. *The Odes and Psalms of Solomon*. 2 vols. Manchester: Manchester University Press, 1916, 1920.
Harris, R. Laird, Gleason L. Archer Jr., Bruce K. Waltke, eds. *Theological Wordbook of the Old Testament*. Chicago: Moody, 1999.
Harrisville, David A. *The Virtuous Wehrmacht: Crafting the Myth of the German Soldier on the Eastern Front, 1941–1944*. Battlegrounds: Cornell Studies in Military History. Ithaca, NY: Cornell University Press, 2021.
Harrisville, Roy A. *The Faith of St. Paul: Transformative Gift of Divine Power*. Eugene, OR: Pickwick, 2019.
———. *Romans*. ACNT. Minneapolis, MN: Augsburg, 1980.
Hawkins, Ralph K. *How Israel Became a People*. Nashville: Abingdon, 2013.
Hays, Richard B. *The Conversion of Imagination: Paul as Interpreter of Israel's Scripture*. Grand Rapids: Eerdmans, 2005.
———. *Echoes of Scripture in the Gospels*. Waco, TX; Baylor University Press, 2016.
———. *Echoes of Scripture in the Letters of Paul*. New Haven, CT: Yale, 1989.
———. "Faith." In *AYBD* 3:1129–33.
Hedrick, Charles W., and Robert Hodgson, Jr., eds. *Nag Hammadi, Gnosticism, and Early Christianity*. Peabody, MA: Hendrickson, 1986.
Hintze, Fritz. "Die Felsenstele Sethos' I. bei Qasr Ibrim." *Zeitschrift für ägyptische Sprache und Altertumskunde* 87 (1962) 31–40.
Hemer, Colin J. "Towards a New Moulton and Milligan." *NovT* 24 (1982) 97–123.
Hengel, Martin. *The Four Gospels and the One Gospel of Jesus Christ*. Translated by John Bowden. Harrisburg, PA: Trinity, 2000.
———. *Judentum und Hellenismus: Studien zu ihrer Begegnung unter besonderer Berücksichtigung Palästinas bis zur Mitte des 2.Jh.s v.Chr*. 2nd ed. WUNT, 10. Tübingen: Mohr Siebeck, 1973.

———. *The Septuagint as Christian Scripture: Its Prehistory and the Problem of Its Canon.* Translated by Mark E. Biddle. Grand Rapids: Baker, 2004.
Heraclitus, *Fragments*. Translated by Brooks Haxton. New York: Viking Penguin, 2001.
Heschel, Susannah. *Aryan Jesus: Christian Theologians and the Bible in Nazi Germany.* Princeton: Princeton University Press, 2010.
Hesse, Franz. *Das Verstockungsproblem im Alten Testament: Eine frömmigkeits geschichtliche Untersuchung.* BZAW 74; Berlin: de Gruyter, 1955.
Hesiod: *The Homeric Hymns and Homerica.* LCL. Translated by Hugh G. Evelyn-White,. 1914. Cambridge: Harvard University Press, 1974.
Hewett, James Allen. *New Testament Greek: A Beginning and Intermediate Grammar.* Rev. ed. with CD by C. Michael Robbins and Steven R. Johnson. Peabody, MA: Hendrickson, 2009.
Hicks, Robert D. *Stoic and Epicurean.* New York: Russell & Russell, 1962.
Hill, Andrew E., and John H. Walton. *A Survey of the Old Testament.* Grand Rapids: Zondervan, 1991.
Hill, Craig C. *Hellenists and Hebrews: Reappraising Division within the Earliest Church.* Minneapolis: Fortress, 1991.
Hinlicky, Paul R. *Before Auschwitz: What Christian Theology Must Learn from the Rise of Nazism.* Eugene, OR: Cascade, 2013.
Hintze, F. "Die Felsenstele Sethos' I. bei Qasr Ibrim." Zeitschrift für ägyptische Sprache und Altertumskunde 87 (1962) 31–40.
Hippocrates. *On Fractures.* Vol. III. Translated by E. T. Withington. LCL. Cambridge: Harvard University Press, 1959. http://classics.mit.edu/Hippocrates/fractur.23.23.html.
Hoffmeier, James K. "Egypt, Plagues of." In *AYBD* 2:374–78.
———. *Israel in Egypt: The Evidence for the Authenticity of the Exodus.* New York: Oxford, 1997.
———. "The Thirteenth-Century (Late Date) Exodus." In *Five Views on the Exodus*, edited by Mark D. Janzen et al., 103–8. Grand Rapids: Zondervan, 2021.
Holmes, Michael W., ed. *The Apostolic Fathers: Greek Texts and English Translations.* 3rd ed. Grand Rapids: Baker, 2007.
Horgan, Maurya P. *Pesharim: Qumran Interpretations of Biblical Books.* The CBQ Monograph Series 8. Washington, DC: Catholic University of America Press, 1979.
Hornblower, Simon, and Anthony Spawforth, ed. *The Oxford Classical Dictionary.* 3rd ed. New York: Oxford University Press, 1996.
Horney, Karen. *Our Inner Conflicts: A Constructive Theory of Neurosis.* New York: Norton, 1992.
Hultgren, Arland J. *Paul's Letter to the Romans: A Commentary.* Grand Rapids: Eerdmans, 2011.
Humphrey, Edith M. "Esdras, Second Book of." In *NIDB* 2:309–13.
Hunt, Arthur S., and C. C. Edgar. *Select Papyri.* 2 vols. LCL. Cambridge: Harvard University Press, 1932.
Hurtado, Larry W. *Lord Jesus Christ: Devotion to Jesus in Earliest Christianity.* Grand Rapids: Eerdmans, 2003.
Iamblichus. *On the Pythagorean Way of Life.* 300 CE. Translated by John Dillon and Jackson Hershbell. Atlanta: Scholars, 1991.
The Interpreter's Dictionary of the Bible, Supplementary Volume. Edited by Keith Crim. Nashville: Abingdon, 1976.

James, William. *The Varieties of Religious Experience*. 1901. Reprint, New York: Penguin, 1982.
Jeffrey, David Lyle, ed. *A Dictionary of Biblical Tradition in English Literature*. Grand Rapids: Eerdmans, 1992.
Jenson, Robert W. *Essays in Theology and Culture*. Grand Rapids: Eerdmans, 1995.
———. *Story and Promise: A Brief Theology of the Gospel of Jesus*. 1973. Reprint, Eugene, OR: Wipf and Stock, 2014.
———. *Systematic Theology: Volume 1: The Triune God*. New York: Oxford University Press, 1997.
———. *Systematic Theology, Volume 2: The Works of God*. New York: Oxford, 1999.
———. "Towards a Christian Theology of Judaism." In *Jews and Christians: People of God*, edited by Carl E. Braaten and R. W. Jenson, 1–13. Grand Rapids: Eerdmans, 2003.
———. *The Triune Identity: God According to the Gospel*. Philadelphia: Fortress, 1982.
Jewett, Robert, and Roy David Kotansky. *Romans: A Commentary*. Hermeneia. Minneapolis: Fortress, 2006.
The Jewish Annotated New Testament: NRSV. Edited by Amy-Jill Levine and Marc Z. Brettler. Oxford: Oxford University Press, 2011. Abbreviation: *JANT*.
Jewish Encyclopedia.com. See online http://www.jewishencyclopedia.com/view.jsp?artid=543&letter=J
Jobes, Karen, and Moises Silva. *Invitation to the Septuagint*. Grand Rapids: Baker, 2005.
Johnstone, William. *Exodus 1–40*. Macon, GA: Smyth & Helwys, 2014.
Joüon, Paul, and T. Muraoka. *A Grammar of Biblical Hebrew*. Roma: Pontificio Istituto Biblico, 2006.
Jung, Carl G. "Approaching the Unconscious." In *Man and His Symbols*, edited by C. G. Jung et al., 1–94. New York: Dell/Random House, 1968.
Juvenal. *Satires with an English Translation*. Edited by G. G. Ramsay. Medford, MA: Heinemann; Putnam's Son, 1918.
Kaiser, Otto. *Isaiah 1–12: A Commentary*. 2nd ed. OTL; Philadelphia; Louisville, KY: Westminster John Knox, 1983.
Kaminsky, Joel, and Mark Reasoner. "The Meaning and Telos of Israel's Election: An Interfaith Response to N. T. Wright's Reading of Paul." *HTR* 112 (2019) 421–44.
Kaminsky, Joel, Joel Lohr, and Mark Reasoner. *The Abingdon Introduction to the Bible: Understanding Jewish and Christian Scriptures*. Nashville: Abingdon, 2014.
Kampen, John. *Hasideans and the Origin of Pharisaism*. SBLCSC. Atlanta: SBL, 1989.
Kaplan, Mordecai M. "Isaiah 6:1–11." *JBL* 45 (1926) 251–59.
Katz, Steven T. "Issues in the Separation of Christianity and Judaism after 70 CE: A Reconsideration." *JBL* 103 (1984) 43–76.
Kee, Howard Clark. *The New Testament in Context: Sources and Documents*. Englewood Cliffs, NJ: Prentice Hall, 1984.
Keener, Craig S. *The Gospel of John: A Commentary*. Volume 1. Peabody, MA: Hendrickson, 2003.
———. *The Gospel of John: A Commentary*. Volume 2. Peabody, MA: Hendrickson, 2003.
Kellenberger, Edgar. "Heil und Verstockung: Zu Jes 6:9f. bei Jesaja und im Neuen Testament." *ThZ* 47 (1992) 268–75.
———. *Die Verstockung Pharaos: Exegetische und auslegungsgeschichtliche Untersuchung zu Exodus 1–5*. BWANT 171. Stuttgart: Kolhammer, 2006.
Kerenyi, Carl. *Dionysos: Archetypal Image of Indestructible Life*. Translated by Ralph Manheim. Princeton, NJ: Princeton University Press, 1976.

Kierkegaard, Søren. *Philosophical Fragments, Johannes Climacus*. Edited and translated by Howard V. Hong and Edna H. Hong. *Kierkegaard's Writings*, vol. VII. Princeton, NJ: Princeton University Press, 1985.

———. *Upbuilding Discourses in Various Spirits*, 1847; edited and translated by Howard V. Hong and Edna H. Hong. Kierkegaard's Writings, vol. XV. Princeton, NJ: Princeton University Press, 1993.

Kille, D. Andrew. *Psychological Biblical Criticism*. GBS. Minneapolis, MN: Fortress, 2001.

Kimelman, Reuven, "Birkat ha-Minim and the Lack of Evidence for an Anti-Christian Jewish Prayer in Late Antiquity." In *Jewish and Christian Self-Definition*, vol. 2: *Aspects of Judaism in the Greco-Roman Period*, edited by E. P. Sanders et al., 226–44. Philadelphia: Fortress, 1981.

Kinzer, Mark S. *Jerusalem Crucified, Jerusalem Risen: The Resurrected Messiah, the Jewish People, and the Land of Promise*. Eugene, OR: Cascade, 2018.

Kirk, G. S. *Heraclitus: The Cosmic Fragments. A Critical Study with Introduction, Text and Translation*. Cambridge: Cambridge University Press, 1954.

Kitchen, K. A. "Egypt, History of: Chronology." In *AYBD* 2:322–31.

———. "Exodus, The." In *AYBD* 2:700–708.

Kittel, Gerhard. "Αἴνιγμα (ἔσοπτρον)." In *TDNT* 1:178–80.

———, and Gerhard Friedrich, eds. *Theological Dictionary of the New Testament*. Translated by Geoffrey W. Bromiley. 10 vols. Grand Rapids: Eerdmans, 1977. Abbrev.: *TDNT*.

Kittel, Rudolf, Karl Elliger, et al. *Torah, Neviim u-Khetuvim. Biblia Hebraica Stuttgartensia*. 5th ed. Stuttgart: Deutsche Bibelstiftung, 1997.

Klein, Charlotte. *Anti-Judaism in Christian Theology*. Translated by E. Quinn; Philadelphia: Fortress, 1978.

Klein, Ralph W. *2 Chronicles: A Commentary*. Hermeneia. Minneapolis: Fortress, 2012.

Klauck, Hans-Josef. *The Religious Context of Early Christianity: A Guide to Graeco-Roman Religions*. Translated by Brian McNeil. Minneapolis: Fortress, 2003.

Kloppenborg, John S. *Q Parallels. Synopsis, Critical Notes, and Concordance*. Sonoma, CA: Polebridge, 1988.

Kloppenborg, John S., and Marvin W Meyer et al. *Q-Thomas Reader*. Sonoma, CA: Polebridge, 1990.

Koehler, Ludwig, et al. *The Hebrew and Aramaic Lexicon of the Old Testament*. Leiden: Brill, 1994–2000. Abbreviation: *HALOT*.

Koester, Craig R. *The Dwelling of God: The Tabernacle in the Old Testament, Intertestamental Jewish Literature, and the New Testament*. CBQMS 22. Washington, DC: Catholic University Press, 1989.

———. *Hebrews*. AYB; New Haven, CT: Yale, 2001.

———. *Symbolism in the Fourth Gospel: Meaning, Mystery, Community*. 2nd ed. Minneapolis: Fortress, 2003.

Köstenberger, Andreas J., and Richard B. Patterson. *Invitation to Biblical Interpretation: Exploring the Hermeneutical Triad of History, Literature, and Theology*. Invitation to Theological Studies Series. Grand Rapids: Kregel Academic & Professional, 2011.

Kristeva, Julia. *Desire and Language: A Semeiotic Approach to Language and Art*. Translated by Leon S. Roudiez et al. European Perspectives Series. Rev. ed. New York: Columbia University Press, 1980.

Lakoff, George, and Mark Johnson. *Metaphors We Live By*. 1980 edition with a new afterword. Chicago: University of Chicago Press, 2003.

BIBLIOGRAPHY

Lamm, Julia A., ed. and trans. *Schleiermacher: Christmas Dialogue, The Second Speech, and Other Selections*. 1806, 1832. New York: Paulist, 2014

Lampe, G. W. H. *A Patristic Greek Lexicon*. New York: Oxford University Press, 1969.

Lanham, Richard A. *A Handlist of Rhetorical Terms*. 2nd ed. Berkeley: University of California Press, 1991.

LaVerdiere, Eugene A. *Introduction to the Pentateuch*. Collegeville, MN: Liturgical, 1971.

Layton, Bentley. *The Gnostic Scriptures: A New Translation with Annotations and Introductions*. The AYB Reference Library. New Haven, CT: Yale University Press, 1995.

Lee, John A. L. *A History of New Testament Lexicography*. Studies in Biblical Greek. Berlin: Lang, 2003.

Leon, Judah Messer. *The Book of The Honeycomb's Flow*. Mantua, Italy, 1475/76. Translated by Isaac Rabinowitz. Ithaca, NY: Cornell, 1980.

Levenson, Jon D. *Death and Resurrection of the Beloved Son*. New Haven, CT: Yale, 1995.

———. "Did God Forgive Adam? An Exercise in Comparative Midrash." In *Jews and Christians: People of God*, edited by Carl E. Braaten and R. W. Jenson, 148–70. Grand Rapids: Eerdmans, 2003.

———. *The Hebrew Bible, The Old Testament, and Historical Criticism: Jews and Christians in Biblical Studies*. Louisville, KY: Westminster John Knox, 1993.

———. "The Universal Horizon of Biblical Particularism." In *Ethnicity and the Bible*, edited by Mark Brett, 143–69. Biblical Interpretation Series. Leiden: Brill, 1996.

Levine, Amy-Jill, and Marc Zvi Brettler, eds. *The Jewish Annotated New Testament: New Revised Standard Version Bible Translation*. New York: Oxford University Press, 2011.

———. *The Misunderstood Jew: The Church and the Scandal of Jewish Jesus*. New York: HarperCollin, 2006.

Lewis, C. S. *The Great Divorce: A Dream*. 1946. Reprint, New York: Harper Collins, 1973.

———. *Surprised by Joy: The Shape of My Early Life*. New York: HBJ, 1955.

Liddell, Henry George, and Robert Scott. *A Greek-English Lexicon*. Revised by Henry Stuart Jones et al. Oxford: Clarendon, 1983. Abbreviation: LSJ.

Lidzbarski, M. *Das Johannesbuch Der Mandäer* 2 pts. 1915. Reprint, St Albans, UK: Wentworth, 2018.

Lightfoot, John. *A Commentary on the New Testament from the Talmud and Hebraica; Matthew—I Corinthians*. 4 vols. 1658. 1859. Reprint, Grand Rapids: Baker, 1979.

Lints, Richard. *Identity and Idolatry: The Image of God and Its Inversion*. New Studies in Biblical Theology 36. Downers Grove, IL: IVP, 2015.

Llewelyn, Stephen R., and R. A. Kearnsley, eds. *New Documents Illustrating Early Christianity. Vol. 7. A Review of the Greek Inscriptions and Papyri published in 1982–83*. North Hyde, NSW: The Ancient History Documentary Research Centre of Macquire University, 1994.

Logos Bible Study Software. Logos Research Systems. See online http://www.logos.com/

Longenecker, Richard N. *Biblical Exegesis in the Apostolic Period*. 2nd ed, Grand Rapids: Eerdmans, 1999.

Louw, Johannes P., and Eugene Albert Nida. *Greek-English Lexicon of the New Testament: Based on Semantic Domains*. New York: United Bible Societies, 1996.

Lundbom, Jack R. "Jeremiah, Book of." In *AYBD* 3:706–21.

Lustiger, Cardinal Jean-Marie. *The Promise* and *Cardinal Jean Marie Lustiger on Christians and Jews*. Grand Rapids: Eerdmans, 2007 (two essays in one volume).

Luther, Martin. *The Bondage of the Will.* Translation of *De Servo Arbitrio* 1525 by J. I. Packer and O. R. Johnston. Old Tappan, NJ: Revel, 1957.

———. "On the Jews and Their Lies" 1543. In *Luther's Works: The Christian in Society IV*, Vol. 47, edited by Franklin Sherman and H. T. Lehmann, 137–306. Philadelphia: Fortress, 1971.

———. "That Jesus Christ Was Born a Jew." 1523. In *Luther's Works: The Christian in Society II*, Vol. 45, edited by Walther I. Brandt and H. T. Lehmann, 200–209. Philadelphia: Fortress, 1962.

Luz, Ulrich. *Matthew 8–20: A Commentary* on Matthew. Translated by J. E. Crouch. Hermeneia. Minneapolis: Fortress, 2001.

MacDonald, Dennis R. ed. *Mimesis and Intertextuality in Antiquity and Christianity.* Harrisburg, PA: Trinity, 2001.

MacRae, George W. *Studies in the New Testament and Gnosticism.* Edited by D. J. Harrington, and S. B. Marrow. 1987. Reprint, Eugene, OR: Wipf and Stock, 2007.

Maier-Katkin, Daniel. *Stranger from Abroad: Hannah Arendt, Martin Heidegger, Friendship and Forgiveness.* New York: Norton, 2010.

Malchow, Bruce V. "Manual for Future Monarchs" *CBQ* 47.2 (1985) 238–45.

Malherbe, Abraham J. *The Cynic Epistles: A Study Edition.* SBLSBS 12. Missoula: Scholars, 1977.

———. *Moral Exhortation: A Greco-Roman Sourcebook.* LEC. Philadelphia: Westminster, 1986.

Malina, Bruce J., and John J. Pilch. *Social-Science Commentary on the Letters of Paul.* Minneapolis: Fortress, 2006.

Malina, Bruce J., and Richard L. Rohrbaugh. *Social Science Commentary on the Synoptic Gospels.* 2nd ed. Minneapolis: Fortress, 2003.

Manson, T. W. *Teaching of Jesus: A Study of Its Form and Content.* 2nd ed. Cambridge: Cambridge University Press, 1935.

Marcos, Natalio Fernandez. *The Septuagint in Context.* Translated by W. G. E. Watson. Leiden: Brill, 1998.

Marcus, Joel. *Mark 1–8.* AYB. New Haven, CT: Yale University Press, 2000.

Margain, Jean. "Causatif et toleratif en Hebreu." *GLECS* 18.23 (1973–1979) 23–31.

Marjanen, Antti, and Petri Luomanen, eds. *A Companion to Second-Century Christian "Heretics."* Leiden: Brill, 2008.

Martin, Ralph P., and David H. Edwards, eds. *Dictionary of the Later New Testament and Its Developments.* IVP Bible Dictionary Series. Downers Grove, IL: IVP Academic, 1997.

Marty, Martin, ed. *The Place of Bonhoeffer.* New York: Association, 1962.

Martyn, J. Louis. *History and Theology in the Fourth Gospel.* Rev. and exp. ed. Louisville, KY: Westminster John Knox, 2003.

Mason, Emma, ed. *Reading the Abrahamic Faiths: Rethinking Religion and Literature.* London: Bloomsbury, 2015.

Mason, Steve. *Flavius Josephus on the Pharisees.* Leiden: Brill, 1991.

———. "Jews, Judaeans, Judaizing, Judaism: Problems of Categorization in Ancient History." *JSJ* 38 (2007) 457–512.

Massumi, Brian. *Parables for the Virtual: Movement, Affect, Sensation.* Durham, NC: Duke University Press, 2002

McDonald, Lee Martin, and James A. Sanders, eds. *The Canon Debate.* Peabody, MA: Hendrickson, 2002.

BIBLIOGRAPHY

———. "Canon of the New Testament." In *NIDB* 1:530–47.
———. "Forming Jewish Scriptures as a Biblical Canon." In *Ancient Jewish and Christian Scriptures*, edited by J. J. Collins et al., 71–96. Louisville, KY: Westminster John Knox, 2020.
———. *Josephus and the New Testament*. Peabody, MA: Hendrickson, 1992.
McGovern, William Montgomery, and Edward McChesney Sait. *From Luther to Hitler: The History of Fascist-Nazi Political Philosophy*. Boston: Houghton Mifflin, 1941.
McKenzie, John L. *A Theology of the Old Testament*. 1974 ed. Reprint, Eugene, OR: Wipf and Stock, 2009.
McLay, R. Timothy. *The Use of the Septuagint in New Testament Research*. Grand Rapids: Eerdmans, 2003.
Meadors, Edward P. *Idolatry and the Hardening of the Heart: A Study in Biblical Theology*. London: T. & T. Clark, 2006.
Meier, John P. *A Marginal Jew, Rethinking the Historical Jesus: Volume Two, Mentor, Message, and Miracles*. New Haven, CT: Yale University Press, 1994.
Menken, M. J. J. *Old Testament Quotations: Studies in Textual Form*. CBET 15. Kampen: Kok, 1996.
Merlan, Philip. *From Platonism to Neoplatonism*. 2nd ed. The Hague: Nijhoff, 1960.
Merriam-Webster's Collegiate Dictionary. 11th ed. Springfield, MA: Merriam-Webster, 2004.
Metzger, Bruce M. *The Bible in Translation: Ancient and English Versions*. Grand Rapids: Baker, 2001.
———. *A Textual Commentary on the Greek New Testament*. 2nd ed. Stuttgart: Deutsche Bibelgesellschaft, 1994.
Metzger, Bruce M., and Bart D. Ehrman. *The Text of the New Testament: Its Transmission, Corruption, and Restoration*. 4th ed. New York: Oxford University Press, 2005.
Meyer, Ben F. "Jesus (Person) Jesus Christ." In *AYBD* 3:773–96.
Meyer, Lester V. "Remnant." In *AYBD* 5:669–71.
Meyers, Jacob M. *I and II Esdras*. AYB. New Haven: Yale University Press, 1974.
Michaels, J. Ramsey. *The Gospel of John*. NICNT. Grand Rapids: Eerdmans, 2010.
Mitchell, David T., and Sharon L. Snyder. *Narrative Prosthesis: Disability and the Dependencies of Discourse*. Ann Arbor, MI: University of Michigan Press, 2001.
Moberly, R. W. L. "Exodus, Book of." In *Dictionary for Theological Interpretation of the Bible*, edited by Kevin J. Vanhoozer et al., 212–13. Grand Rapids: Baker Academic, 2005.
Moloney, Francis J. *The Gospel of Mark: A Commentary*. Grand Rapids: Baker Academic, 2012.
Morgan, Michael L. ed. *A Holocaust Reader: Responses to Nazi Extermination*. New York: Oxford University Press, 2001.
Moulton, James Hope, et al. *A Grammar of New Testament Greek*. 4 vols. Edinburgh: T. & T. Clark, 1908–76. Vol. 1 (1908) *Prolegomena*, by J. H. Moulton, 1st ed. (1906); 3d ed. (1908). Vol. 2 (1929) *Accidence and Word Formation*, by Wilbert Francis Howard. Vol. 3 (1963) *Syntax*, by Nigel Turner; Vol. 4 (1976) *Style*, by Nigel Turner.
Moulton, James Hope, and George Milligan. *The Vocabulary of the Greek Testament*. 1930. Reprint, Grand Rapids: Eerdmans, 1980.
Moulton, William F., Alfred S. Geden, and Harold K. Moulton, eds. 6th rev., edited by I. Howard Marshall. *A Concordance to the Greek New Testament*. Edinburgh: T. & T. Clark, 2004.

Munk, Elie. *The Call of the Torah. An Anthology of Interpretation and Commentary on the Five Books of Moses.* Brooklyn, NY: Shemos, 1994.

Muraoka, Takamitsu. *Hebrew/Aramaic Index to the Septuagint. Keyed to the Hatch-Redpath Concordance.* Grand Rapids; Baker, 1998.

Myers, Alicia D., and Bruce G. Schuchard. *Abiding Words: The Use of Scripture in the Gospel of John.* Resources for Biblical Study 81. Atlanta: SBL, 2015.

Myers, Charles D., Jr. "Romans, Epistle to the." In *AYBD* 5:816–30.

Nanos, Mark. "'Broken Branches': A Pauline Metaphor Gone Awry? (Romans 11:11–36)." In *Between Gospel and Election: Explorations in the Interpretation of Romans 9–11*, edited by Florian Wilk et al., 339–76. Tübingen: Mohr Siebeck, 2010.

———. "'Callused', Not 'Hardened': Paul's Revelation of Temporary Protection until All Israel Can Be Healed." In *Reading Paul in Context: Explorations in Identity Formation*, edited by Kathy Ehrensperger et al., 52–73. London: T. & T. Clark, 2010.

———. *Reading Romans within Judaism.* Vol. 2. Eugene, OR: Cascade, 2018.

———. "Romans: Introduction and Annotations." *JANT*, 253–86.

NET Bible. *The New English Translation.* 1st ed. Biblical Studies Press, 2005. www.bible.org.

Neusner, Jacob, trans. *The Babylonian Talmud.* 50 vols. Peabody, MA: Hendrickson, 2008–11.

———. *Introduction to Rabbinic Literature.* New Haven, CT: Yale University Press, 1994.

———. *The Mishnah: A New Translation.* New Haven, CT: Yale University Press, 1988.

———. *Rabbinic Judaism: Structure and System.* Minneapolis: Fortress, 1995.

———, trans. *The Tosefta: Translated from the Hebrew with a New Introduction.* 2 vols. Peabody, MA: Hendrickson, 2002.

Neusner, Jacob, and William Scott, eds. *Dictionary of Judaism in the Biblical Period: 450 B.C.E to 600 C.E.* 1996. Peabody, MA: Hendrickson, 1999.

Neusner, Jacob, and Alan Avery-Peck, and William Scott Green, eds. *The Encyclopedia of Judaism.* 2nd ed. Leiden: Brill, 2005.

New Documents Illustrating Early Christianity. Vols. 1–9. A Review of the Greek Inscriptions and Papyri published in 1976–87 (in separate vols.). Edited by G. H. R. Horsley, S. R. Llewelyn, et al. The Ancient History Documentary Research Centre of Macquire University, North Ryde, N.S.W., Australia, 1981–2002. Grand Rapids: Eerdmans, 1998–2002.

A New English Translation of the Septuagint and the Other Greek Translations Traditionally Included under That Title. Edited by Albert Pietersma and Benjamin G. Wright. New York: Oxford University Press, 2007.

The New Interpreter's Dictionary of the Bible. 5 vols. Edited by Katharine Doob Sakenfeld et al. Nashville: Abingdon, 2006–9.

The New Jerome Biblical Commentary. Edited by Raymond E. Brown, Joseph A. Fitzmyer, Roland E. Murphy. Englewood, Cliffs, NJ: Prentice Hall, 1990.

Nickelsburg, George W. *Ancient Judaism and Christian Origins: Diversity, Continuity, and Transformation.* Minneapolis: Fortress, 2003.

———. *1 Enoch.* Hermeneia. Minneapolis: Fortress, 2001.

———. *Jewish Literature between the Bible and the Mishnah: A Historical and Literary Introduction.* Minneapolis: Fortress, 2005.

Nida, Eugene A. "The Implications of Contemporary Linguistics for Biblical Scholarship." *JBL* 91 (1972) 73–89.

BIBLIOGRAPHY

Nilsson, Martin P. *The Dionysiac Mysteries of the Hellenistic and Roman Age*. Lund: Gleerup, 1957.

Nock, A. D., and A. J. Festugiére. *Corpus Hermeticum*, vol. 1, Poimandrés, Traités 1–12; vol. 2, Traités 13–18, Asclépius. Paris: College de Universités, 1945.

Noonan, Benjamin J. *Advances in the Study of Biblical Hebrew and Aramaic: New Insights for Reading the Old Testament*. Grand Rapids: Zondervan Academic, 2020.

Noth, Martin. *The Deuteronomistic History*. 1958. Reprint, Sheffield, UK: JSOT, 1981.

Novak, David. "Theology and Philosophy: An Exchange with Robert Jenson." In *Trinity, Time & Church: A Response to the Theology of Robert W. Jenson*, edited by Colin Gunton, 42–61. Grand Rapids: Eerdmans, 2000.

———. "From Supersessionism to Parallelism in Jewish-Christian Dialogue." In *Jews and Christians: People of God*, edited by Carl E. Braaten and Robert W. Jenson, 95–113. Grand Rapids: Eerdmans, 2003.

Novum Testamentum Graece. Edited by Eberhard and Erwin Nestle, Barbara and Kurt Aland, et al. 28th ed. Stuttgart: Bibelgesellschaft, 2012.

Ong, Walter J. "A Writer's Audience Is Always a Fiction." In his *Interfaces of the Word: Studies in the Evolution of Consciousness and Culture*, 53–81. Ithaca, NY: Cornell University Press, 1977.

Oswalt, John N. *The Book of Isaiah, Chapters 1–39*. NICOT. Grand Rapids: Eerdmans, 1986.

O'Toole, Robert F. "Why Did Luke Write Acts (Luke-Acts)?" *Biblical Theology Bulletin* 7 (1977) 66–76.

Oxford Latin Dictionary. Edited by P. G. W. Glare. 2 vols. 2nd ed. Oxford: Oxford University Press, 2012.

Paget, James Carleton. "The Definition of the Terms *Jewish Christian* and *Jewish Christianity* in the History of Research." In *Jewish Believers in Jesus: The Early Centuries*, edited by Oskar Skarsaune and Reidar Hvalvik, 22–52. Peabody, MA: Hendrickson, 2007.

Paley, William. *A View of the Evidences of Christianity in Three Parts*. London: W. T. Warren, n.d.

Palmer, Micheal. A Comprehensive Bibliography of Hellenistic Greek Linguistics see online, http://www.greek-language.com/Palmer-bibiography.html.

Pannenberg, Wolfhart. *Anthropology in Theological Perspective*. Translated by M. J. O'Connell. Philadelphia: Westminster, 1985.

Parry, Donald W., and Emanuel Tov, eds. *The Dead Sea Scrolls Reader*. 6 vols.; Leiden: Brill, 2004.

Patrologia Graeca. Edited by J.-P. Migne. 162 vols. Paris, 1857–86.

Patrologia Latina. Edited by J.-P. Migne. 217 vols. Paris, 1844–64.

Paul, Shalom M. *Isaiah 40—66*. Grand Rapids: Eerdmans, 2012.

Pearson, Donn. *Cool Hand Luke*. New York: Scribners, 1965.

Penchansky, David. *The Politics of Biblical Theology*. Studies in American Biblical Hermeneutics. Macon, GA: Mercer University Press, 1995.

———. *Solomon and the Ant: The Qur'an in Conversation with the Bible*. Eugene, OR: Cascade, 2021.

———. *Understanding Wisdom Literature: Conflict and Dissonance in the Hebrew Text*. Grand Rapids: Eerdmans, 2012.

Philo, with an English Translation. Edited by F. H. Colson; G. H. Whittaker; and R. Marcus. 10 vols and 2 supplementary vols. LCL. Cambridge: Harvard University Press, 1929–62.

BIBLIOGRAPHY

Piankoff, Alexandre. *Le "coeur" dans les textes Égyptiens: Depuis l'Ancien jusq'à la fin du Nouvel Empire*. Paris: Librairie Orientaliste Paul Geuthner, 1930.

Pickthall, Mohammed Marmduke. *The Meaning of the Glorious Koran*. New York: Penguin, 1983.

Pilch, John. *The Cultural Dictionary of the Bible*. Collegeville, MN: Liturgical, 1999.

Pinnock, Clark. "God Limits His Knowledge." In *Predestination and Free Will: Four Views of Divine Sovereignty & Human Freedom*, edited by David Basinger and Randall Basinger, 141–62. Downers Grove, IL: IVP, 1986.

Plato: Euthyrphro, Apology, Crito et al. Translated by Harold North Fowler, 1914. Vol. 1 of 12. LCL. Cambridge: Harvard University Press, 2005.

———. *Lysis, Symposium, Gorgias*. Translated by W. R. M. Lamb, 1932. Vol. 3 of 12. LCL. Cambridge: Harvard University Press, 1983.

———. *Theaetetus, Sophist*. Vol. 7. Translated by H. N. Fowler. LCL. Cambridge: Harvard University Press, 1921.

———. *Timaeus, Critias* et al. Translated by R. G. Bury, 1929. Vol. 7 of 12. LCL. Cambridge: Harvard University Press, 1961.

Porter, Stanley E., ed. *The Criteria for Authenticity in Historical-Jesus Research: Previous Discussions and New Proposals*. JSNTSup 91; Sheffield, UK: Sheffield Academic Press, 2000.

———, ed. *Hearing the Old Testament in the New Testament*. Grand Rapids: Eerdmans, 2006.

———, ed. *The Language of the New Testament: Classic Essays*. Sheffield, UK: Sheffield Academic Press, 1991.

Porter, Stanley E., and Dennis L. Stamps, eds. *Rhetorical Criticism and the Bible*. London: Sheffield Academic, 2002.

Pratt, D. Butler. "The Gospel of John from the Standpoint of Greek Tragedy." *Biblical World* 30 (1907) 448–59. https://www.psychologytoday.com/us/basics/defense-mechanisms.

Pury, Albert de. "Yahwist Source." In *AYBD* 6:1012–19.

Puskas, Charles B. *The Conclusion of Luke-Acts: The Significance of Acts 28:16–31*. Eugene, OR: Pickwick, 2009.

Puskas, Charles B. *Hebrews, the General Letters, and Revelation: An Introduction*. Eugene, OR: Cascade, 2016.

Puskas, Charles B., and C. Michael Robbins. *The Conceptual Worlds of the Fourth Gospel: Intertextuality and Early Reception*. Eugene, OR: Cascade, 2021.

Puskas, Charles B., and David Crump. *An Introduction to the Gospels and Acts*. Grand Rapids: Eerdmans, 2008.

Puskas, Charles B., and Mark Reasoner. *The Letters of Paul: An Introduction*. 2nd ed. Collegeville, MN: Liturgical, 2013.

Puskas, Charles B., and C. Michael Robbins. *An Introduction to the New Testament*. 2nd ed. Eugene, OR: Cascade, 2011.

The Qur'an. Translated by M. H. Shakir. Elmhurst, NY: Tahrike Tarsile Qur'an, 1993.

Rad, Gerhard von. *Deuteronomy: A Commentary*. Translated by D. Barton. OTL. Philadelphia: Westminster, 1966.

———. *Old Testament Theology*. OTL. 2 vols. Translated by D. M. G. Stalker. Louisville, KY: Westminster John Knox, 1962, 1965.

Rahlfs, Alfred, et al., ed. *Septuaginta: id est vetus testamentum graece juxta LXX interpretes.* Stuttgart: Würtemberg Bible Society, 1935. Rev. ed. by Robert Hanhart. 2 vols. in one. Stuttgart: Deutsche Bibelgesellschaft, 2006.

Rashkover, Randi, and Martin Kavka, eds., *Tradition in the Public Square: A David Novak Reader* Grand Rapids: Eerdmans, 2008.

Reasoner, Mark. *Five Models of Scripture.* Grand Rapids: Eerdmans, 2021.

Reichenbach, Bruce. "God Limits His Power." In *Predestination and Free Will: Four Views of Divine Sovereignty & Human Freedom.* Edited by David Basinger and Randall Basinger, 99–124. Downers Grove, IL: IVP, 1986.

Reinhartz, Adele. *Cast Out of the Covenant: Jews and Anti-Judaism in the Gospel of John.* Lanham, MD: Lexington Fortress Academic, 2018.

Reitzenstein, Richard. *Hellenistic Mystery Religions: Their Basic Ideas and Significance.* Translated by John E. Steely. Pittsburgh: Pickwick, 1978.

———. *Poimandres: Studien zur Grieschisch-Ägyptischen und Frühchristlichen Literatur.* 1904. Reprint, Darmstad: Wissenschaftliche Buchgesellschaft, 1966.

Rendsburg, Gary A. *How the Bible Was Written.* Peabody, MA: Hendrickson, 2019.

———. "Response to James K. Hoffmeier (The Twelfth-Century Exodus View)." In *Five Views on the Exodus: Historicity, Chronology, and Theological Implications,* edited by Mark D. Janzen et al., 121–23. Counterpoints Bible and Theology. Grand Rapids: Zondervan Academic, 2021.

Reventlow, Henning Graf. "Theology (Biblical), History of." Translated by F. H. Cryer. In *AYBD* 6:483–505.

Ricoeur, Paul. *The Symbolism of Evil.* Translated by E. Buchanan. Religious Perspectives 7. Boston: Beacon, 1967.

Riley, Gregory J. *One Jesus, Many Christs. How Jesus Inspired Not One True Christianity, But Many.* New York: Harper San Francisco, 1997.

———. *The River of God: A New History of Christian Origins.* New York: Harper San Francisco, 2001.

Rist, J. M. *Stoic Philosophy.* Cambridge: Cambridge University Press, 1969.

Rist, Martin. "Pseudepigraphy and the Early Christians." In *Studies in NT and Early Christian Literature,* edited by David Aune, 3–24. Leiden: Brill 1972.

Roberts, J. J. M. *First Isaiah: A Commentary.* Hermeneia; Minneapolis: Fortress, 2015.

Robbins, C. Michael. *The Testing of Jesus in Q.* Berlin: Lang, 2007.

Robinson, James M., gen. ed. *The Nag Hammadi Library.* Rev. ed. New York: Harper Collins, 1990.

Robinson, H. Wheeler. *Corporate Personality in Ancient Israel.* 1964. Reprint, Philadelphia: Fortress, 1973.

Rogerson, John W. *Old Testament Criticism in the Nineteenth* Century. Minneapolis: Fortress, 1984.

Ronning, John. *The Jewish Targums and John's Logos Theology.* 2010. Reprint, Grand Rapids: Baker Academic, 2011.

Rosenbaum, M.D., Jean. *The Mind Factor: How Your Emotions Affect Your Health.* New York: Prentice-Hall, 1973.

Rosenthal, Michael. *Nicholas Miraculous: The Amazing Career of the Redoubtable Dr. Nicholas Murray Butler.* New York: Farrar, Straus and Giroux, 2006.

Routledge, R. L. "Blessings and Curses." In *DOTP,* 61–67.

Rubenstein, Richard L. *After Auschwitz: Radical Theology and Contemporary Judaism.* Indianapolis: Bobbs-Merrill, 1966.

Rudolph, Kurt. *Gnosis: The Nature and History of Gnosticism*. Translated by Robert McLachlan Wilson. New York: HarperCollins, 1987.
Ryken, Leland, et al., eds. *Dictionary of Biblical Imagery*. Downers Grove, IL: IVP, 1998.
Ryle, H. S., and M. R. James. *Psalmoi Solomontos: Psalms of the Pharisees*. Cambridge: Cambridge University Press, 1891.
Salmon, Marilyn J. *Preaching without Contempt: Overcoming Unintended Anti-Judaism*. Minneapolis: Fortress, 2006.
Sanders, E. P. *Jesus and Judaism*. London: SCM, 1985.
———. *Jewish Law from Jesus to the Mishnah: Five Studies*. Harrisburg, PA: Trinity, 1990.
———. *Paul and Palestinian Judaism: A Comparison of Patterns of Religions*. Philadelphia: Fortress, 1977.
Sandmel, Samuel. *Judaism and Christian Beginnings*. New York: Oxford University Press, 1978.
Saussure, Ferdinand de. *Course in General Linguistics*. Edited by C. Bally, A. Sechehaye et al. Translated by Wade Baskin. New York: Columbia University Press, 2011.
Schaps, David. *Handbook for Classical Research*. London: Routledge, 2009.
Schiffmann, Lawrence H., and James C. Vanderkam, eds. *Encyclopedia of the Dead Sea Scrolls*. 2 vols. Oxford: Oxford University Press, 2000.
———. *Texts and Traditions. A Source Reader for the Study of Second Temple and Rabbinic Judaism*. Hoboken, NJ: KTAV, 1998.
Schneemelcher, Wilhelm, ed. *New Testament Apocrypha*. Rev. ed. Vol. 1. *Gospels and Related Writings*. Vol. 2. *Writings Related to the Apostles, Apocalypses, and Related Subjects*. Translated by R. McL. Wilson. Rev. ed. Louisville, KY: Westminster John Knox, 2003.
Schnelle, Udo. *The Human Condition*. Translated by O. C. Dean. Minneapolis: Fortress, 1996.
———. *Theology of the New Testament*. Translated by M. Eugene Boring. Grand Rapids: Baker Academic, 2009.
Schuchard, Bruce G. *Scripture within Scripture: The Interrelationship of Form and Function in the Explicit Old Testament Citations in the Gospel of John*. SBLDS 133. Atlanta: Scholars Press, 1992.
Scullion, John J. "God: God in the Old Testament." In *AYBD* 2:1041–48.
Seale, David. *Vision and Stagecraft in Sophocles*. Chicago: University of Chicago, 1982.
Searle, John R. *Speech Acts: An Essay in the Philosophy of Language*. New ed. Cambridge: Cambridge University Press, 1970.
Segal, Alan. "Mysticism." *EDEJ* 982–86.
Seitz, Christopher R. "Handing Over the Name: Christian Reflection on the Divine Name." In *Trinity, Time and Church: A Response to the Theology of Robert W. Jenson*, edited by Colin Gunston, 23–41. Grand Rapids: Eerdmans, 2000.
———. *Zion's Final Destiny: The Development of the Book of Isaiah*. Minneapolis: Fortress, 1991.
Seneca: Moral Essays I: De Providentia, De Constantia, De Ira, De Clementia. Translated by John W. Basore. LCL. Cambridge: Harvard University Press, 1928.
Shanks, Hershel, ed. *Christianity and Rabbinic Judaism: A Parallel History of Their Origins and Early Development*. Washington, DC: Biblical Archaeology Society, 1992.
Shirun-Grumach, Irene. *Untersuchungen zur Lebenslehre des Ameno*. Munich: Deutscher Kunstverlag, 1972.

BIBLIOGRAPHY

Siemon-Netto, Uwe. *The Fabricated Luther: Refuting Nazi Connections and Other Modern Myths*. St. Louis, MO: Concordia, 2007.

Silva, Moises. *Biblical Words and Their Meaning: An Introduction to Lexical Semantics*. 1983. Reprint, Grand Rapids: Zondervan, 1994.

Silverman, David P., ed. *Ancient Egypt*. New York: Oxford University Press, 1997.

Skarsaune, Oskar, and Reidar Hvalvik, eds. *Jewish Believers in Jesus: The Early Centuries*. Peabody, MA: Hendrickson, 2007.

Skinner, Christopher W., ed. *Characters and Characterization in the Gospel of John*. LNTS 461. London: T. & T. Clark, 2013.

———. *John and Thomas—Gospels in Conflict? Johannine Characterization and the Thomas Question*. Princeton Theological Monograph Series 115. Eugene, OR: Pickwick, 2009.

Slayton, Joel C. "Sihon (Person)." In *AYBD* 6:22.

Smith, Gary V. *Isaiah 1–39*. NAC. Nashville: Broadman and Holman, 2007.

Smith, Jonathan Z. *Drudgery Divine: On the Comparison of Early Christianities and the Religions of Late Antiquity*. Jordan Lectures on Comparative Religion, 14. Chicago: University of Chicago, 1990.

Smith, Mark S. *Exodus*. New Collegeville Bible Commentary. Collegeville, MN: Liturgical, 2011.

Sommer, Benjamin D. *A Prophet Reads Scripture: Allusion in Isaiah 40–66*. Stanford, CA: Stanford University Press, 1998.

Soulen, Richard N., and R. Kendall Soulen. *Handbook of Biblical Criticism*. 4th ed. Rev. and exp. ed. Louisville, KY: Westminster John Knox, 2011.

Soulen, R. Kendall. *The God of Israel and Christian Theology*. Minneapolis: Fortress, 1996.

———. "Hallowed Be Thy Name! The Tetragrammaton and the Name of the Trinity." In *Jews and Christians: People of God*, edited by Carl Braaten and Robert Jenson, 14–40. Grand Rapids: Eerdmans, 2003.

———. "Karl Barth and the Future of the God of Israel." *Pro Ecclesia* 6 (1997) 413–28.

———. "YHWH The Triune God." *Modern Theology* 15.1 (1999) 25–54.

Spicq, Ceslas. "σκληροκαρδία, σκληρός." In *Theological Lexicon of the New Testament*, Vol 3, edited by Celas Spicq et al., 258–62. Peabody, MA: Hendrickson, 1994.

Stanley, Christopher D. *Paul and the Language of Scripture. Citation Technique in the Pauline Epistles and Contemporary Literature*. SNTSMS 74. Cambridge: Cambridge University Press, 1992.

Steck, Odil H. "Bemerkungen zu Jesaja 6." *BZ* 16 (1972) 188–206.

Stegemann, Hartmut, ed. *The Library of Qumran: On the Essenes, Qumran, John the Baptist, and Jesus*. Grand Rapids: Eerdmans, 1998.

Steinmann, Andrew E. "Hardness of Heart." In *Dictionary of the Old Testament: Pentateuch*, edited by T. D. Alexander and D. W. Baker, 381–82. Downers Grove, IL: IVP Academic, 2003.

Stenmans, Peter. "כָּבֵד κτλ." In *TDOT* 7:13–22.

Stevens, Anthony. *Jung*. Past Masters Series. New York: Oxford University Press, 1994.

Storr, Anthony. *Freud*. Past Masters Series. New York: Oxford University Press, 1989.

Strack, Hermann L., and G. Stemberg. *Introduction to the Talmud and Midrash*. Translated by Markus Bockmuehl. Edinburgh: T. & T.Clark, 1991.

Strack, Hermann L., and Paul Billerbeck. *Kommentar zum Neuen Testament aus Talmud und Midrasch*. 6 vols. Munich: Beck, 1922–61.

BIBLIOGRAPHY

Stuckenbruck, Loren T. *Angel Veneration and Christology: A Study in Early Judaism and in the Christology of the Apocalypse of John.* Wissenschaftliche Untersuchungen zum Neuen Testament. 2nd Series 70. Tübingen: Mohr, 1995.

———. "Apocrypha and Pseudepigrapha." *EDEJ* 143–62.

———. "An Approach to the New Testament through Aramaic Sources: The Recent Methodological Debate." *JSP* 8 (1991) 3–29.

———. *The Myth of Rebellious Angels: Studies in Second Temple Judaism and New Testament Texts.* Grand Rapids: Eerdmans, 2014.

Sussman, Max. "Sickness and Disease." *AYBD* 6:6–15.

Sweeney, Marvin. *Isaiah 1–39: With an Introduction to Prophetic Literature.* FOTL, 16. Grand Rapids: Eerdmans, 1996.

Swidler, Leonard, Khalid Duran, Reuven Firestone, eds. *Trialogue: Jews, Christians, and Muslims in Dialogue.* New London, CT: Twenty-Third, 2007.

Tal, Uriel. *Christians and Jews in Germany: Religion, Politics and Ideology in the Second Reich, 1870–1914.* Ithaca, NY: Cornell University Press, 1975.

Tate, W. Randolph. *Biblical Interpretation: An Integrated Approach.* Grand Rapids: Baker, 1991.

———. *Interpreting the Bible: A Handbook of Terms and Methods.* Grand Rapids: Baker, 2006.

Taylor, Charles. *Sources of the Self: The Making of the Modern Identity.* Cambridge: Harvard University Press, 1989.

Taylor, Walter F., Jr. "Humanity, New Testament View of." In *AYBD* 3:321–25.

Tertullian. *Liber De Anima.* Edited by Jan Hendrik Waszink. 1933 ed. Leiden: Brill, 2009.

———. *Treatise on the Soul.* Translated by Peter Holmes. In *ANF* 3:181–236.

Thandeka. *The Embodied Self: Friedrich Schleiermacher's Solution to Kant's Problem of the Empirical Self.* SUNY Series in Philosophy. Albany, NY: State University of New York, 1995.

Thayer, Joseph Henry. *A Greek-English Lexicon of the New Testament.* 1889. Reprint, *Thayer's Greek-English Lexicon of the New Testament.* Peabody, MA: Hendrickson, 1996.

Theological Lexicon of the New Testament. 3 vols. Translated and edited by James D. Ernest from *Notes de lexicographie néo-testamentaire,* edited by Ceslas Spicq. 1978. Peabody, MA: Hendrickson, 1994.

Thesaurus Linguae Graecae: A Digital Library of Greek Literature. University of California, Irvine. See online http://www.tlg.uci.edu/

Thesaurus Linguae Latinae. Bayerische Akademie. Manfred Flieger, Sec. See online http://www.thesaurus.badw.de/english/index.htm

Thiselton, Anthony C. *Hermeneutics: An Introduction.* Grand Rapids: Eerdmans, 2009.

———. "Semantics and Biblical Interpretation." In *New Testament Interpretation,* edited by I. H. Marshall, 75–104. Grand Rapids: Eerdmans, 1977.

———. *Thiselton on Hermeneutics. Collected Works with New Essays.* Grand Rapids: Eerdmans, 2006.

Thompson, Marianne Meye. *The God of the Gospel of John.* Grand Rapids: Eerdmans, 2001.

———. *John: A Commentary.* NTL. Louisville, KY: Westminster John Knox, 2015.

Tigay, Jeffrey H. "On the Tolerative/Permissive Hiphil." In *Le-Ma'am Ziony: Essays in Honor of Ziony Zevit,* edited by Frederick E. Greenspan and Gary A. Rendsburg, 397–414. Eugene, OR: Cascade, 2017.

BIBLIOGRAPHY

Tillich, Paul. *Systematic Theology, Vol. 2. Existence and the Christ*. Chicago: University of Chicago Press, 1957.

Torrey, Charles Cutler. *The Four Gospels: A New Translation*. New York: Harper, 1933.

Torsten, Uhlig. *The Theme of Hardening in the Book of Isaiah: An Analysis of Communicative Action*. Forschungen Zum Alten Testament 2. Tübingen: Mohr Siebeck, 2009.

Tov, Emanuel. *Textual Criticism of the Hebrew Bible*. 3rd ed. rev. and exp. Minneapolis: Fortress, 2012.

Throntveit, Mark A. *Ezra-Nehemiah*. Interpretation. Louisville, KY: Westminster John Knox, 1992.

Trebolle, Julio. "Canon of the OT." *NIDB* 1:548–63.

VanderKam, James C., and Peter W. Flint. *The Meaning of the Dead Sea Scrolls: Their Significance for Understanding the Bible, Judaism, Jesus, and Christianity*. New York: HarperSanFrancisco, 2002.

van der Woude, A. S. " קשׁה qšh, to be hard." In *Theological Lexicon of the Old Testament*, Vol. 3, edited by Ernst Jenni and Claus Westermann, 1175–76. Peabody, MA: Hendrickson, 1997.

Van Seters, John. *Abraham in History and Tradition*. New Haven, CT: Yale, 1975.

Vanhoozer, Kevin J. *Is There a Meaning in This Text?* Grand Rapids: Zondervan, 1998.

Via, Dan O. *The Hardened Heart and Tragic Finitude*. Eugene, OR: Cascade, 2012.

Volf, Miroslav. *Exclusion and Embrace: A Theological Exploration of Identity, Otherness, and Reconciliation*. Nashville: Abingdon, 1996.

Walsh, Robyn Faith. *The Origins of Early Christianity: Contextualizing the NT within Greco-Roman Culture*. Cambridge: Cambridge University Press, 2020.

Waltke, Bruce. *Proverbs, Chapters 15:30—31:31*. NICOT. Grand Rapids: Eerdmans, 2005.

Walton, John H. "Retribution." In *Dictionary of the Old Testament: Wisdom, Poetry & Writings*, edited by Tremper Longman III and Peter Enns, 647–55. Downers Grove, IL: IVP, 2008. Abbreviation: *DOTW*.

Warfield, B. B. "PREDESTINATION." In *A Dictionary of the Bible: Dealing with Its Language, Literature, and Contents Including the Biblical Theology, Vol. 4*, edited by James Hastings et al., 47–63. New York: Scribner's Sons, 1911–12.

Wassertein, Abraham, and David Wassertein. *The Legend of the Septuagint. From Classical Antiquity to Today*. Cambridge: Cambridge University Press, 2006.

Watson, Duane F. "Angels: New Testament." *AYBD* 1:253–55.

Wead, David W. *The Literary Devices in John's Gospel*. 1970. Rev. ed. Edited by Paul N. Anderson and R. Alan Culpepper. Johannine Monograph series. Eugene, OR: Wipf and Stock, 2018.

Weber, C. P. "חזק" In *Theological Workbook of the OT*, Vol. 1, edited by R. Laird Harris et al., 276–77. Chicago: Moody, 1980.

Weber, Robert, et al., eds. *Biblia Sacra Vulgata: Iuxta Vulgatem Versionem*. 4th ed. Stuttgart: Deutsche Bibelgesellschaft, 1994.

Westermann, Claus. ed. *Essays in Old Testament Hermeneutics*. Translated by J. L. Mays. Atlanta: John Knox, 1963.

Whybray, Roger N. *An Introduction to the Pentateuch*. Grand Rapids: Eerdmans, 1995.

Wildberger, Hans. *A Continental Commentary: Isaiah 1–12*. Translated by T. H. Trapp. Minneapolis: Fortress, 1991.

Williams, Clifford. *The Divided Soul: A Kierkegaardian Exploration*. Eugene, OR: Wipf & Stock, 2009.

Williams, M. H. "The Expulsion of the Jews from Rome in A.D. 19." *Latomus* 48 (1989) 765–84.
Wilson, Robert R. "The Hardening of Pharaoh's Heart." *CBQ* 41 (1979) 19–21.
Winston, David. *The Wisdom of Solomon*. AYB 43. New Haven, CT: Yale, 2008.
Wolff, Hans Walter. *Anthropology of the Old Testament*. Philadelphia: Fortress, 1974.
Wolff, Hans Walter, and Bernd Janowski et al. *Anthropologie des Alten Testaments*. Gütersloh: Gütersloher Verlagshaus, 2010.
Wright, N. T. *The Climax of the Covenant: Christ and the Law in Pauline Theology*. Minneapolis: Fortress, 1991.
———. *The New Testament and the People of God*. Christian Origins and the Question of God. Minneapolis: Fortress, 1992.
———. *Paul and the Faithfulness of God*. Minneapolis: Fortress, 2013.
Wünch, Hans-Georg. "The Strong and the Fat Heart." *OTE* 30.1 (2017) 165–88.
Wyschogrod, Michael. *The Body of Faith: God in the People of Israel*. San Francisco: Harper & Row, 1983.
Yamauchi, Edwin M. *Mandean Incantation Texts*. AOS 49. New Haven, CT: Yale University Press, 1967.
———. *Pre-Christian Gnosticism: A Survey of the Proposed Evidences*. 2nd ed. Baker, 1983. Reprint, Eugene, OR: Wipf and Stock, 2003.
Zimmerli, Walther. *Ezekiel 1*. A Commentary on the Book of the Prophet Ezekiel, Chapters 1–24. Translated by R. E. Clements. Hermeneia. Minneapolis: Fortress, 1979.

Author Index

Allison, Dale C., 36n9
Arnold, B. T., 12n27
Attridge, Harold W., 47n52
Austin, J. L., 17n50, 48n55, 59n37

Beltzer, Klaus, 23n78
Barr, James, 6n5, 33–34, 60n41
Barrett, C. K., 20n63
Barth, Karl, 38n17, 61n3, 66n232, 69n32
Bauer, Walter, 25n86, 41–42
Beale, G. K., 39n21, 57n30
BeDuhn, Jason D., 65n19
Black, Matthew 37n14
Blenkinsopp, Joseph 12n26
Block, Daniel I., 25, 56
Braaten, Carl E., 62, 65, 66–67, 69
Brown, Alexandra, 48n55
Brueggemann, W. 28, 52n8
Bultmann, Rudolf, 3n10, 34n6, 44n39, 57n28

Calvin, John, 13n32
Cameron, J. M., 11n21
Cassidy, Richard, 39n20
Cassuto, Umberto, 10, 11n20, 12n27
Celsus, 43n35, 59, 74n46
Ceresko, Anthony, 27n93
Charles, R. H., 21n66

Charlesworth, James, 44n40
Childs, Brevard S., 10–12
Chomsky, Noam, 74n47
Christensen, Duane, 16n47
Clayton, Philip, 54n14
Clère, J. J., 12n25
Coats, George W., 9n16
Cohen, Shaye J. D., 68n28
Collins, John J., 5n1, 33n1, 68n28
Conrad, Edgar, 32n105
Cook, Michael, 72n42
Cox, Dorian J. C., 7n7
Craigie, Peter C., 25–26
Cullmann, Oscar, 3n10
Cunningham, Philip, 63n7, 69n30
Currid, John D., 7n7, 15n38

Danker, Frederick, 18n52
Dann, Moshe, 10n18, 54n17
Davies, W. D., 36n9, 73n43
deClaissé-Walford, 10n17
Dodd, C. H., 37n13
Dozemann, Thomas, 7n8, 12–13, 55n19
Driver, Samuel R., 12
Dunn, James D. G., 43n35, 59n39, 73–74

Eichrodt, Walther, 14n34, 24n81, 56n22, 75n50

Eising, Hermann, 10n18
Elliott, John H., 41n27
Enns, Peter, 13n33
Erasmus, Desiderius, 13n32, 53n11, 55n20
Ericksen, Robert P., 64
Erman, Adolf, 12n25
Evans, Craig, 19–20, 33n3, 36n11, 42, 51–52, 74n45

Feinberg, John S., 14n34, 54
Feldmeier, Reinhard, 75n50
Fensham, F. Charles, 31n103
Fitzmyer, Joseph A., 72n42
Ford, William A., 12n29
Fowler, Robert M., 2n2, 38n16, 45n43
Fretheim, Terence E., 12n26, 16–17
Freud, Sigmund, 2n3
Furnish, Victor Paul, 42n31

Gadamer, H.-G., 64
Gamble, Harry Y., 33n1, 53n10
Garland, David E., 41
Garrett, Duane A., 12n28
Garroway, Joshua, 68n28
Gnilka, Joachim, 33n3
Goldingay, John, 4n10, 22, 44n41
Gritsch, Eric W., 63n11
Gunton, Colin, 67–68
Gupta, Nijay K., 52n8

Hanauer, Ned, 74n47
Harmon, Matthew, 22n69
Harnack, Adolf von, 65n19
Harrisville, David, 2n4
Harrisville, Roy A., 42n32
Harrisville, R. A., III, xvi
Hastings, James, 53
Hawkins, Ralph K., 9n15
Hays, Richard B., 52n8
Heschel, Susannah, 64–65
Hesse, Franz, 3n10, 6n6, 14n34, 74n45
Hill, Andrew E., 14n37
Hill, Craig C., 36n9
Hinlicky, Paul R., 64
Hintze, Fritz, 12n25
Hoffmeier, James, 9n15, 15n39

Horney, Karen, 3n5
Hultgren, Arland J., 73
Humphrey, Edith M., 31n104
Hurtado, Larry W., 36n9

James, William, 3n5
Jenson, Robert W., 40n23, 60–75
Jewett, Robert, 43n34, 48n53
Johnstone, William, 14n35
Jung, Carl G., 2n3, 58n35

Kaiser, Otto, 18
Kaminsky, Joel, 40n23, 43n36, 60
Kaplan, Mordecai, 18n54, 58n35
Katz, Steven T., 44n40
Kellenberger, Edgar, xvi, 7n7, 13n32, 18n54, 21n67, 53n11
Kierkegaard, Soren, 2–3, 38n34
Kille, D. Andrew, 2–3
Kimelman, Reuven, 44n40
Kinzer, Mark S., 40n22
Kitchen, K. A., 9n15, 10n17
Kittel, Gerhard 34n3, 52n9, 64
Klein, Charlotte, 64–65
Klein, Ralph W., 30
Koester, Craig R., 47

Lakoff, George, 8n12, 57n27
Lamm, Julia A., 3, 56–57
LaVerdiere, E. A., 12–13
Leon, Judah Messer., 22n70
Levenson, Jon D., 65n20, 72, 75n50
Levine, Amy-Jill, 68n28
Lewis, C. S., 13n32, 16n45
Lints, Richard, 24n79
Louw, Johannes P., 34n4, 50n1, 57n30
Lundbom, Jack R., 59n38
Lustiger, Jean-Marie, 71n38
Luther, Martin, 13n32, 23n77, 53, 55n20, 63–64, 67n26, 74n45
Luz, Ulrich, 40n26

Maier-Katkin, D., 64n12
Malchow, Bruce V., 29
Maline, Bruce M., 38n19, 68n28
Manson, T. W., 37n14
Marcus, Joel. 36–38, 45n43

AUTHOR INDEX

Margain, Jean, 13n33, 54n15
Martyn, J. Louis, 44n40
Mason, Emma, 76n51
Mason, Steve, 41n27
Massumi, Brian, 8n12, 57n27
McDonald, Lee M., 5n2, 33n1
McGovern, W. M., 64n13
Meador, Edwin P., 23, 25, 29, 53, 56n25
Meier, John P., 45n45
Meyer, Ben F., 38n18
Meyer, Lester V., 32n105
Meyers, Jacob M., 31n104
Mitchell, David T., 30n102
Moberly, R. W. L., 15n42
Moloney, Francis J., 44–45
Morgan, Michael L., 65
Munk, Elie, 10n18, 54n17
Muraoka, Takamitsu, 13n33
Myers, Charles D., 42n33

Nanos, Mark, 34, 43, 59, 62, 73–74, 76
Neusner, Jacob, 56n22, 70n35
Nida, Eugene A., 34n4, 50n1, 57n30
Novak, David, 62n4, 65–67, 74–75

Oswalt, John N., 19n59, 50n1, 59n40
O'Toole, Robert F., xv-xvi, 39n21

Paley, William, 50–51
Parry, Robin, xvi
Paul, Shalom, 24
Pearson, Donn, 1n1
Penchansky, David, xvi, 6n5, 8n11
Piankoff, Alexandre, 12n25
Pickthall, M. M., 20n61
Pilch, John, 68n28
Pinnock, Clark, 53–54
Pury, Albert de, 9n14
Puskas, Charles B., xv, 22n72, 36–37, 39–40, 44n40, 46, 57n36, 66n20

Rad, Gerhard von, 4, 9n14, 26n90, 64, 75n50
Rahlfs, Alfred, 5n2, 12n30
Rashkover, Randi, 75n49
Reasoner, Mark, xvi, 35n8, 40n23, 43n36, 46–47, 60, 72

Reichenbach, Bruce, 54n13
Reitzenstein, R., 20n63
Rendsburg, Gary A., 9n15
Reventlow, H. G., 4n10
Ricoeur, Paul, 55n21
Robbins, C. M., 22n72, 44n40
Roberts, J. J. M., 19n56, 20n63
Robinson, H. W., 18n54, 69n29
Rogerson, John W., 12n27
Rosenbaum, Jean, 11n21
Rosenthal, Michael, 64n12
Routledge, R. L., 17n50
Rubenstein, R. L., 65
Ryken, Leland, 8n12, 21n65, 57n27

Salmon, Marilyn J., 66n22
Saussure, F. de, xv, 6n3
Schnelle, Udo, 34n6, 37n12, 41n28, 57n28
Scullion, John J., 32n106
Seale, David, 20n60, 43n37
Seale, J. R., 59n37
Seitz, Christopher R., 67–68
Shirun-Grumach, I., 12n25
Siemon-Netto, Uwe, 64n13
Silva, Moises, 6
Silverman, David P., 7n7
Slayton, Joel C., 15n43
Smith, Gary V., 18n54
Sommer, Bejamin D., 23n78
Soulen, Richard N., 46n47
Soulen, R. Kendall, 64, 66–67, 69–70
Spicq, Ceslas, 8n11, 33n3, 57n29
Stanley, Christopher, 43n34, 48n53
Steck, Odil H., 18n55
Steinmann, Andrew, 7–8, 14n34, 25n87, 55n18
Stenmans, Peter, 18n53
Stuckenbruck, Loren 5n2, 42n31
Sussman, Max, 11n21
Sweeney, Marvin, 16n47, 18–21
Swidler, Leonard, 76n51

Tal, Uriel, 65n16
Tate, W. Randolph, xvi
Taylor, Charles, 3n7, 57n31

AUTHOR INDEX

Thiselton, Anthony, xv-xvi, 6, 17n50, 33–34, 48n54, 59–60
Thompson, M. M., 43n37
Throntveit, Mark, 31n103
Tigay, Jeffrey H., 13n33, 24n81, 54n15
Torsten, Uhlig, 18n54, 23n78
Trebolle, Julio, 5n1

van der Woude, A., 23n75
Van Seters, John, 13m31
Via, Dan O., 2n4, 14n36, 55
Volf, Miroslav, 25–26, 45

Walsh, Robyn F., 36n9
Waltke, Bruce, 28–29
Walton, John H., 14n37, 28n96

Warfield, B. B., 14n34, 53n12
Watson, Duane F., 2n2
Weber, C. P., 14n34
Westermann, Claus, 64, 75n50
Whybray, Roger N., 12n26
Wildeberger, Hans, 19–20
Wilson, Robert R., 11–12
Winston, David, 14n37, 16n46
Wolff, Hans Walter, 11n22, 41n28
Wright, N. T., 43n36, 60–61, 63n10, 72n42
Wünch, Hans-Georg, 11n22
Wyschogrod, M., 74

Zimmerli, Walther, 24n83, 25n85

Ancient Document Index

Old Testament

Genesis

1:3–5	45
1:27	45
2:4b—3:24	3
3	2
3:15	63
8:21b	19
9:26	9
15:18	9
17:14	7
18:18–33	70
19:11	17, 21, 25
20:17	13, 70
21:12c	74
25:23	9
25:26	23
27:36	23
27:37	9
27:40	9
48:10	7
49:10f	63

Exodus

1–15	9
1–24	12
4–14	10–11, 15, 54–55
4:4	54
4:11	17
4:14	54
4:21	10, 54
5:2	14
5:23	14
7:3	55
7:8–13	15
7:11	14
7:13	13, 55
7:14—12:30	10
7:14	12–13, 55
7:17	15
7:22	13
8:15	12–13, 47
8:19	14
8:22	12
8:32	12, 47
9:7	12–13

ANCIENT DOCUMENT INDEX

Exodus (continued)

9:12	10, 13, 54
9:16	10, 15
9:34	12, 47
9:35	13
10:1–2	12–13
10:20	10, 13, 54
10:27	13
11:10	10, 13, 55
12–15	17
12:36	13
13:9	10
13:14–16	15
14:4	10, 13, 15, 55
14:17	13, 55
14:17–18	15
16:4	37
19:6	72
20–24	17
20:5	21
23:8	17, 25
24:7	41
25—31	12
29:12	14
32	17
32–34	12
33	17
33:3	34, 57
33:5	8, 16, 34, 39, 57
34:9	57
34:16	19
35–40	12

Leviticus

23:23–24	72
26	24
26:1	56
26:1–2	14
26:41	39

Numbers

12:2	13
12:6	13
20:1–13	29

Deuteronomy

1:38	55
2:30	13, 15, 25
3:28	55
4:37	10
8:20	11
9:6	29
9:13	29
9:23	28
9:29	10
10:16	23, 26, 29, 39, 47
15:7	25
16:19	17, 21, 25
20:8	11
27–28	27
28:3	22
29:2–29	26
29:3	22, 25–26, 48
29:4	26
29:17–19	26
29:18	26
29:28	26
30:6	26, 39
30:15–20	23, 53
31:7	55
31:27	17, 27
31:33	55
32	27
32:15–17	27
32:39	27

Joshua

2:8–14	16
7:5	11
11:20	15
23:6	55

Judges

9:23	27

1 Samuel

2:25	27
6:6	12, 15, 27
15:9	19

ANCIENT DOCUMENT INDEX

18:6–11	27
18:10	27
19:9–11	27
24:16–17	27
25:37	11
28:15–19	27

1 Kings

15:13	26
21:19	28
22	24
22:1–38	28
22:19–23	18–20
22:20	20

2 Kings

3:27–27	32
6:18	17, 21, 25
6:20	17, 25
9:24	11
17:14	29, 47
19:2	53
21:10–16	30
23:3	18
23:26–27	30
23:32	30
24:3–4	30
25:7	17, 21, 25, 30
25:27	32

2 Chronicles

30:8	47
34:15–20	53
36:11–17	30
36:12–13	32
36:13	30, 32

Nehemiah

9	27, 31–32
9:1—10:39	31
9:16–17	30, 47, 57
9:25	19
9:26	30
9:29	30, 47, 57
9:35	19

Job

4:7	52
9:24	21
12:13–25	28
25:4–6	28

Psalms

2:1–3	14
12:2	58
22	37
22:15	11
23 LXX	52
24:4	52
41:9	37
51:10	52
68 LXX	29, 42
69	29
69:23–24	29, 32
77 LXX	37
78:8	29
78:24	37
78:40, 56	29
78:42–51	10
80:13	28
81:13	29
85	32
94 LXX	30, 33, 49, 76
95	49, 76
95:8	29
95:7–11	29–30, 37
105:28–36	10
106:13–33	29
115	24–25
115:4–8	25–26, 32
117 LXX	37
118:25–26	37
119:70	19
135	24–25
135:15–18	25, 32

ANCIENT DOCUMENT INDEX

Proverbs

20:12	17
21:24	28
24:32	22
28:14	28–29
28:28—29:2	29, 32
29:1	32

Ecclesiastes

7:29	23
8:14—9:4	28

Isaiah

1:17	21
1:21	21
1:25–26	21
1:29–30	21
5:7	19
5:18–23	20
6:1–13	18–20
6:9–10	18–22, 24–26. 29, 31, 33–34, 36–37, 39, 43–48, 58–59
6:10	13, 17, 19
6:12–13	21
6:13	32
7:2	11, 18, 58
7:14	63
7:17	18, 58
8:17	21
9:13–21	74
10:5	16
10:12	16
10:19	32, 71
10:20–21	32
10:20–23	21
11:11–12	32
14:4ff	16
19:14	16, 20
25:6–8	52
26:11	21
28:7–8	20
29:9a	17, 21
29:9–10	19–20, 26, 41–42
30:1–3	20
30:2–21	22
31:1	21
32:3–4	22
35:3–5	22, 32
35:5	21, 39
37:31–32	70
37:36–38	16
40:3	37
42:6	39
42:7	21
42:16	21
42:18–19	21, 32
42:18–20	23
43:5–7	32
43:8–11	21–23
44:9	23, 32
44:18	23, 32
46:3–4	32, 71
48:4	23
48:4–5	32
48:8–11	23
49:6	37, 39
49:53	37
50:7	23
52:10	39
56:6–8	72
56:10	21, 32
57:13a	24
57:17–18	24
57:19–21	24
59:10	17
59:15b–20	32
60:3	39
61:1	22
63:1–6	32
63:17	24, 32
64:1–3	32
64:7	24, 29
66:3–4	23
66:20–21	32, 71

Jeremiah

1:12	59
3:17	26
4:4	23, 26, 39, 57

4:28	59	36:26	25
5:3	57	39:28	71
5:3–5	23		
5:17–18	26	*Daniel*	
5:19–23	56		
5:20–31	22, 32	9:24ff	63–64
5:21	22, 25, 35		
5:23	35	*Hosea*	
6:10	39, 57		
7:24	23, 29	4:16	23
7:26	47	11:8	24
7:27	22		
7:31–32	22–23	*Amos*	
8:5	24		
9:13	29	1:3—2:16	16
9:25	39, 57	1:8	71
16:12	23, 35	5:1–3	16
17:9	23	5:3	21
17:23	47	6:9	21
18:11–12	23	8:1–3	16
23:3	32, 70	9:1–2	71
25:15–16	31	9:13–21	21
27:1–28:12	23		
29:10–14	23	*Micah*	
31:7–8	32, 71		
31:31–34	59	4:7	71
39:7	17, 21, 25		
44:4–5	23	*Habakkuk*	
46—51	16		
50:45	53	1:13	52
52:11	17, 21, 25		
		Zephaniah	
Ezekiel			
		3:11–13	32
2:3–4	25		
2:3—3:9	32	*Zechariah*	
2:4	57		
3:7–9	25, 57	1:7–17	18
9:8	32, 71	7:11	56
11:13	32, 71	7:12	47
11:19–21	25, 71	9:1–17	32
12:2	22, 25, 32	10:1–12	32
20:38	21	11:3–5	24
33:6	32	12:10	37
34:2–4	24	14:4	32
36:22–32	74		
36:25–28	59		

Malachi

3:16–18	32

Apocrypha and Pseudepigrapha

Tobit

13:6	53

Wisdom of Solomon

10:16	14
12:3–11	16
12:3–18	16
13:1–9	35
15:15	56

Sirach/Ecclesiasticus

1:28	3, 58
16:11	34
30:8	29
33:11-13	42
36 LXX	23

1 Maccabees

2:70	63

2 Maccabees

6:6	68

2 Esdras/4 Ezra

7:22–24	31
7:26–30	31
14:45–47	5n1

1 Enoch

91:4	3, 58
99:8–9	56

Jubilees

8:8–11	16
9:14–15	16
10:29–34	16
22:17–18	56

Epistle of Jeremiah

6:64	56

Testament of Judah

19:4	42

New Testament

Matthew

3:8–9	40
5:8	52
5:44	45
13:10–13	40
13:10–17	58
13:13	40
13:14–15	37, 40
13:16–17	40
15:3–6	38
16:16	36
18:15–20	36
19:1–12	38
19:8	38
28:19	36

Mark

1:1—8:26	37
1:16–20	45
1:33	63
3:5	36
3:13—6:6a	37–38
3:13–19	45
4:10	45
4:11–12	36–38, 49
4:12	52
4:13	45
4:23	45

ANCIENT DOCUMENT INDEX

4:40–41	45	8:16–18	39
5:16	45	8:18	40
5:31	45	24:27	39
6:5	49	24:44–48	36
6:7–30	45		
6:25	36		
6:30–44	45	*John*	
6:37	45	1:1–4	44
6:52	45	1:11	43
7:10–12	38	1:14	43
7:17–18	37	1:18	43
7:32–35	45	1:34	43
8:1–10	46	1:38–39	43
8:4	45	1:46	43
8:11–21	45	3:16–17	44, 52
8:17–18	36–37, 45, 49	4:42	44
8:21	45	6:14	44
8:22–26	45–46, 49	8:12	44
8:27—10:52	37	9:5	44
8:27–33	46, 49	9:22	44
8:34–38	46	9:39	43, 48
9:9–13	46	11:35	43
9:31–32	46	12:32	52
10:1–12	38	12:39	43
10:5	34, 38	12:40	43, 48
10:33–34	46	12:42	44
10:43	46	12:47	44
10:46–52	46	14:9	43
10:52	49	16:2	44
11:1—16:8	37	20:25	43
11:23	37	20:28–31	36
14:22–25	36	20:29	43
15:36–39	46	20:30–31	36
16:6–7	46		
16:14	45	*Acts*	
		2:14–42	39
Luke		4:28	54
1:1–4	36	7:51	57
1:69–70	40	7:51–53	39
2:32	39	13:44–47	39, 48, 59
3:8	40	15:5	40
4:18	39	17:1	39
4:25–28	39	17:4	39
7:22	39	17:12	39
8:9–10	58	18:5	59
8:10	48, 52, 59	18:6	39, 48

Acts (continued)

18:8	39–40
19:8–9	59
19:9	47
23:6	39–40
27:27	59
28	48
28:23–28	39
28:24a	40
28:25–27	41
28:26	52
28:26–28	58–59
28:28	39
28:30	40

Romans

1:5	60
1:18	35, 47
1:21–23	34–35, 47
1:24	35
1:26	35
1:28	34, 57
2:5	47
3:23–24	45
5:12–21	72
7:15	58
8:29–30	54
9–11	42, 73
9:4	72
9:1–5	42
9:6–29	42, 60
9:17–18	42, 72
9:27–29	42, 71
9:30—10:21	42
11:1–36	42
11:5	40, 74
11:7–8	41, 52
11:13–24	40
11:17–18	76
11:17–20	62, 73
11:24	72
11:25	41–43, 72
11:25–29	43, 48, 59
11:26–27	40, 48, 63, 72
11:28–29	73
11:33	72
13:9–10	60
15:9–13	43, 60

1 Corinthians

1–2	48
1:10–11	46, 49
2:6	42
2:7	54
2:8	42
5:12–13	38
9:20	73
11:23–26	36
13:12	52
15:28	52

2 Corinthians

3:3	48
3:13	41
3:14–16	41–42
4:3–4	41–42
4:4	41–42
5:19	52
13:5	46

Galatians

1:6	46, 49
3–4	73
3:1–5	46
3:4–5	49
3:36–39	72
5:6	73

Ephesians

1:5	54
1:10	52
1:11	54
2:2	42
3:1–5	46
4:17–18	34–35, 57
4:25—5:21	35

Colossians

4:5	38

1 Thessalonians

4:12	38

2 Thessalonians

2:9–11	28

1 Timothy

2:4	52
3:7	38
4:19	52

Titus

2:11	52

Hebrews

3:5–6	47
3:7–8	45
3:8	30, 34, 47, 57
3:8—4:7	49
3:12–13	38
3:15	30, 47, 76
4:7	30, 47
7:16	25

James

1:8	2, 58
4:8	2

2 Peter

2:1–22	46
3:9	52

1 John

1:10	46
2:4	46
2:19	46
2:26	46
4:20	46

Revelation

2:4	46
3:15	46
22:14–15	38

Dead Sea Scrolls

CD (Cairo Genizah)

III.10–16a	31

1QH (Thanksgiving Hymn)

V.36	38

Isaiah Scroll

IQ Isa[a]	59

1QS (Community Rule)

I.24–25	31
III.15–21	42
IV.2–18	40

11Q11 (Apocryphal Psalms)

V.6–7	42

Hellenistic Jewish Writings

Philo

De confusion linguarum

171–82	42

De ebrietate

108	34

Quod omnis probus liber sit

175–91	41n27

Josephus

Against Apion
1.37–41	5n1
2.38–39	41n27

Jewish Antiquities
11.173	68n28
18.11–12	41n27
20.38–39	68n28

Jewish War
2.119	41n27

Rabbinic Writings

Avot de R. Natan
4.5	70

b. Berakot
1a	70
28b	70

b. Sukkah
51b	70

Exodus Rabbah
13.3	55

m. Megillah
4.8	38

m. Pirkei Avot
3.15a	56

Greek and Roman Writings

Celsus
De Medicina	43n35, 59, 74n46

Galen

Ars Medica
1.387	43n35, 59, 74n46

Hippocrates

De Fractures
23.10	43n35, 59, 74n46
	43n35, 59, 74n46

De Articulus
15.6	43n35, 59, 74n46

Iamblichus

Pythagoras	38n19

Sophocles

Antigone	55
Oedipus Rex	14n36, 55

Gnostic and Early Christian Writings

Apocalypse of James (NHL I 2)
7.1–7	38

Apocalypse of Peter
73:11–17	40

Epistle of Diognetus
11–13	46

Second Clement
13:1	38

Testimony of Truth (NHL IX 3)
48.8–15	40

www.ingramcontent.com/pod-product-compliance
Lightning Source LLC
Chambersburg PA
CBHW030902170426
43193CB00009BA/708